Union Public Library
1980 Morris Avenue
Union, N.J. 07083

D1175422

THE GOURMET'S GUIDE TO

COOKING WITH

LIQUORS AND SPIRITS

THE GOURMET'S GUIDE TO
COOKING WITH

LIQUORS AND SPIRITS

Extraordinary Recipes Made with Vodka,
Rum, Whiskey, and More!

Union Public Library
1980 Morris Avenue
Union, N.J. 07083

DWAYNE RIDGAWAY

BEVERLY MASSACHUSETTS

QUARRY BOOKS

© 2010 by Quarry Books

All rights reserved. No part of this book may be reproduced in any form without written permission of the copyright owners. All images in this book have been reproduced with the knowledge and prior consent of the artists concerned, and no responsibility is accepted by the producer, publisher, or printer for any infringement of copyright or otherwise, arising from the contents of this publication. Every effort has been made to ensure that credits accurately comply with information supplied. We apologize for any inaccuracies that may have occurred and will resolve inaccurate or missing information in a subsequent reprinting of the book.

First published in the United States of America by
Quarry Books, a member of
Quayside Publishing Group
100 Cummings Center
Suite 406-L
Beverly, Massachusetts 01915-6101
Telephone: (978) 282-9590
Fax: (978) 283-2742
www.quarrybooks.com

Library of Congress Cataloging-in-Publication Data
Ridgaway, Dwayne.
    The gourmet's guide to cooking with liquors and spirits : extraordinary recipes made with vodka, rum, whiskey, and more! / Dwayne Ridgaway.
        p. cm.
    Includes index.
    ISBN-13: 978-1-59253-594-1
    ISBN-10: 1-59253-594-1
    1. Cookery (Liquors) I. Title.
    TX726.R54 2010
    641.6'25--dc22

                                                                2010008998
                                                                CIP

Cover Design: Sussner Design Company.
Page Layout: Claire MacMaster,
    barefoot art graphic design/deepwater-creative.com
Photography: Glenn Scott Photography
Food Styling: Liz Walkowicz

Printed in China

**Coconut Rum Key Lime Cake,
page 186**

Contents

Introduction

If you're like me, your liquor cabinet seems to grow and grow every year. Every occasion seems to have a special drink that goes along with it. There was the summer of Cosmopolitans, and the year of the Apple Martini. Espresso Martinis, Mojitos—with all of these specialty cocktails comes the overstocked bar. This leaves little room for the *well-stocked* bar that everyone should have.

With this book at your side, dust off some of those bottles and start using up your stock—in the kitchen! Added to any dish in the right quantity at the right time, spirits can enhance the flavor of any food.

Soon you'll start to think of liquors and spirits as extensions of the spices and herbs in your spice rack: simple sources of flavor for your cooking. (So many of these beverages are distilled from botanicals and organic material that they are nearly spices themselves.)

For more than three thousand years, people have produced spirits for medicinal and recreational purposes. In modern times, it is almost universally customary to have a drink before, during, or after dinner. Many cultures produce aperitifs and digestifs, but few traditions have married the two as I do in this book. Sure, wine and fortified wines have been used to cook with for hundreds of years, but seldom do you see coffee liqueur or Midori used in the kitchen.

The Gourmet's Guide to Cooking with Liquors and Spirits is full of fantastic dishes, from breakfast to dessert and everything in between, using all of your favorites and some obscure choices in celebration of liquors and spirits. For some, wine may be as far as the liquor and culinary pairing will go. Classic French cooking teaches us that wines and fortified wines are the traditional alcohol addition to foods. Let's pop the cork on that theory and agree that flavor is flavor, whether it comes from classic wines or from a unique liqueur.

The Spirited Kitchen

The Nature of Liquors and Spirits

Spirits are created from the fermentation of organic products such as fruits and grains, which are distilled into alcohol. These fruits and grains enter a still as a liquid solution and are boiled to condense the alcohol vapors. Boiling the liquid reduces the overall volume and increases the percentage of alcohol in the mixture. This is where alcohol by volume (ABV) percentages, such as 40% ABV (or 80 proof), are determined.

LIQUOR OR LIQUEUR?

There are distinct differences between *spirits*, *liquors*, and *liqueurs*. As noted above, **spirits** is the general term for alcoholic beverages that are produced by the natural distillation of corn, rye, wheat, barley, beets, sugar cane, grapes, and so on. **Liquors** are unsweetened spirits whose flavors are determined solely by their base ingredients during the distillation and aging process. Whiskey, vodka, and rum are all liquors. For our purposes, flavored vodkas (and for that matter, flavored rums, gins, and tequilas) will be considered spirits. **Liqueurs**, also known as *cordials*, are sweetened or spiced, spirits grouped by their flavor profile. Additionally, some liqueurs may have a slightly syrupy consistency compared to other spirits. Many liqueurs use finished spirits such as whiskey, cognac, and rum as their base, adding new ingredients, such as macerated fruit, to create a new profile. *Schnapps* is a generic term (not a brand name) given to an array of flavored and white spirits that originated in the northern European regions of Germany and Scandinavia. There is a fine line between flavored vodkas and schnapps, but that varies by country. Other generic liqueurs include those of a particular flavor, such as crème de menthe and curaçao, which can be made by many different producers. Proprietaries are trademarked liqueurs that are produced

Anise by Any Other Name

Pernod, ouzo, and sambuca are clear spirits that all have similar flavor profiles yet with unique botanical qualities that give them subtle differences. All three are anisettes, a generic spirit derived from anise. Pernod is from France; ouzo is from Greece; and sambuca, from Italty.

according to specific guidelines as dictated by their producer and include Grand Marnier, Goldschläger, and Southern Comfort.

Liquor and Spirit Flavor Profiles

Understanding flavor profile is essential to choosing a liquor for cooking. Consider first the ingredients being used and how they come together in the recipe, and then break down your desired spirit to its basic flavor profiles before incorporating it into the recipe. Many foods are easily labeled as sweet or savory, but many popular liquors and spirits are not sorted into such black-and-white categories.

CLEAR LIQUORS AND SPIRITS

Vodka is the result of fermenting and then distilling the simple sugars from a mash of grain or vegetables. It is the predominant spirit in the cultures of Eastern Europe, most notably in Russia. Russian vodka is made from wheat, whereas its counterpart in Poland uses potatoes. France produces vodkas from grapes, and Sweden is known for its wheat mash vodkas. Vodka is a clear spirit with little to no true distinctive flavor, and it is used in cooking mostly for the effect its base distillate has on the flavor. Whether grain, corn, potato, or grape derived, a subtle flavor will be added to a dish when cooking with vodka.

In recent years, **flavored vodkas** have arrived with a vengeance: vodkas flavored with the extracts of pepper, watermelon, vanilla, and chocolate dominate the shelf with as much marketing thrust as flavor. Also, a niche of makers even include such nontraditional ingredients as cucumber and tomato during the distillation process of their vodka. This process flavors the vodka naturally, using the actual plant and not an extract. These unique, natural flavor profiles can be incorporated into your cooking. You can also infuse ready-made unflavored vodka with your own ingredients, to produce a unique flavor. (See page 42 for recipes for making infused vodkas at home, including Tomato Vine, Rosemary, Tea, and Berry.)

Gin gets its distinctive flavor from the juniper berry, added to its primary spirit base of grain, usually rye or wheat. Gin is the most herbal and floral of spirits; other botanicals used in its production process may include orange peel, coriander, anise, cinnamon, angelica root, and other organic plant matter. The combination of or the amount of botanicals is solely dependent on the maker. Certain proprietors (including Tanqueray, Seagram, Hendrick, and Bombay) have developed their own recipes for their products. Seagram's gin, for example, has a distinctive lime foreground and juniper finish, whereas Tanqueray and Hendrick's are subtly sweet with a cucumber finish. Because of the variety of botanicals used in the making of gins, from flower blossoms to bark, they are a tremendous flavoring element for cooking.

Rum is made from distilling fermented cane sugar (usually as molasses) and water. Molasses, which is more than 50 percent sugar, contains minerals and other trace elements that contribute in part to the final taste of the spirit. There are five categories of rums: white, golden, dark, spiced, and añejo.

- White rums are typically used as mixers, and are the most widely used rums in bar-mixed drinks. Having very little flavor profile, white or light rums are usually clear and very subtle in their flavors (unless they are aged).
- Golden rums are medium-bodied. They are aged for several years in oak casks, producing a smooth, delicate flavor.
- Dark rums are bolder, fuller bodied, and more caramel-like in their flavor and color, and are typically aged in oak barrels longer than golden rums are.
- Spiced rums are white, golden, and dark rums that have been infused with spices and fruits, varying by producer.
- Añejo ("aged") rums, aged in oak barrels for even longer than dark rums, have become more popular in recent years and are often "sipped" like a fine whiskey or scotch. Aged rums may comprise several vintages that are mixed together from year to year to maintain continuity within a label.

MEDIUM-BODIED AND AMBER SPIRITS

This broad category of spirits includes **dark and spiced rums**, **brandies and cognacs**, **whiskeys and scotches**, and **aged and rested tequilas**. All these spirits have a common thread: their flavors are more intense, more pronounced, and deeper than their light or clear counterparts. Dark and spiced rums have caramel notes with a hint of bark and smoke. Brandies and cognacs have notes of vanilla, citrus, and spice, and some even have a foreboding note of black pepper. Whiskeys and scotches are the most intense of all the amber spirits, and can even be harsh, with leather, smoke, or tobacco aromas. Whiskeys and scotches are heavy and need a bold dish to handle them.

Tequila

Tequila is distilled from the juice of the agave plant, a long, spiky-leaved succulent in the lily family. Blue agave (*Agave tequilana*), by Mexican law, is the only agave allowed to make true tequila and likewise can only be produced in specifically designated geographic areas, primarily in the west-central Mexican state of Jalisco. Tequila is mostly a clear or white spirit but may have a golden hue, due to either the addition of caramel or aging. There are four categories of tequila: silver, gold, reposado, and añejo.

- Silver tequila (*plata*, a.k.a. white/*blanco*) is clear with little or no aging at all. Silver tequilas are used primarily for mixing into fruit drinks.
- Gold tequila (*oro* or *joven*) is unaged silver tequila with caramel added for color and flavor.
- Reposado ("rested") is aged tequila. Reposado tequila is typically aged in wooden casks for a minimum of two months.
- Añejo ("old") is aged in wooden barrels (often, used previously for bourbon) for a minimum of twelve months, sometimes for eighteen months to three or four years.

The last two tequilas are called for most often in these recipes due mostly to the flavor profiles the two offer. Most if not all the flavor in tequila comes from the aging process in wooden barrels or casks. Many of the characteristics unique to the agave plant are removed during the distillation process.

... and a Bottle of Rum

Rums hail mostly from island and tropical regions, and most of the recipes in this book that include rum are ones that have a balance of island flavor and tropical vibe. Barbados, Cuba, Martinique, and Jamaica, among others, export rums, the flavor profiles of which can be as unique as the islands themselves. Barbados is the home of Mount Gay Distillery, which produces a light, sweet rum. Martinique, a department of France, makes rums from both cane juice and molasses, and some of these rums are aged in old brandy casks for three years; Martinique's rums are frequently compared to French brandies.

Whiskey / Bourbon

Whiskeys (including Tennessee, rye, and Canadian variations) are spirits made from grains, including corn, rye, wheat, and barley, combined in different proportions and aged differently depending on the specific whiskey. The aging can occur for varied periods of time in old or new barrels, charred or uncharred, again depending on the type of whiskey being made. Irish whiskey is a triple-distilled whiskey made in Ireland from fermented barley; that same grain is smoked first over a peat fire to make the distinctively flavored Scotch whisky. Bourbon is an American whiskey that contains at least 51 percent corn as its grain; it is then aged in new oak barrels for at least two years.

Cooking with Liquors and Spirits

Kitchen wisdom teaches us that alcohol burns off during cooking. Alcohol content is diminished by cooking, but the percentage varies from alcohol to alcohol. The fact is, not all the alcohol ever cooks off, regardless of which type of cooking or baking is being done. Also a fact: More alcohol is burned off during simmering or baking than when flamed over a pan.

Below is a simple table (developed by the U.S. Department of Agriculture) that indicates how much alcohol is retained (not burned off) in foods after cooking.

PREPARATION METHOD	PERCENT OF ALCOHOL RETAINED
Alcohol added to boiling liquid and removed from heat	85%
Alcohol flamed	75%
No heat used in cooking, stored overnight	70%
Baked for 25 minutes, alcohol not stirred into mixture	45%

BAKED OR SIMMERED DISHES WITH ALCOHOL STIRRED INTO MIXTURE

15-minute cooking time	40%
30-minute cooking time	35%
1-hour cooking time	25%
1½-hour cooking time	20%
2-hour cooking time	10%
2½-hour cooking time	5%

When you are cooking with any alcohol, always keep your guests in mind. These retained percentages may be significant to recovering alcoholics, parents (and parents-to-be), and those who may have ethical or religious reasons for avoiding alcohol. That said, alcohol is a naturally occurring element in many foods, especially fruits with a high sugar content, such as a ripe apple. Also, the small amount of the spirit used in a dish is minimal compared to the volume of the rest of ingredients. Although this cannot override anyone's beliefs or ethics regarding the use of alcohol, it should reassure cautious guests who are concerned with just how much alcohol a dish contains.

FLAMBÉ (FLAMING)

Alcohol is a flammable liquid. No recipes in this book call for flambéing (or flaming) because of the inherent danger that fire poses in your home kitchen. Yes, flambéing is a theatrical, beautiful way to present several classic dishes prepared with spirits, but I don't encourage people to use the technique in their kitchen unless they have been instructed on the proper way to do so. I do encourage creative exploration in the kitchen, but always with caution and with regard for your surroundings. Flambéing can be particularly dangerous on or near a gas stovetop. Always use caution when cooking with alcohol.

Nutritional Facts about Spirits

Speaking in general terms, simply focusing on actual distilled spirits and not those that are considered infusions or "flavored," spirits, I offer the following nutritional facts regarding alcohol. They have been determined by considering the proof of the spirit or the alcohol by volume (ABV) that is generally indicated on the beverage label.

1 jigger (1.5 ounces, or 42 ml) of 80-proof liquor (40% ABV), such as gin, rum, vodka, or whiskey

97 calories

0 g protein

0 g fat

0 g carbohydrate

14 g alcohol

1 jigger (1.5 ounces, or 42 ml) of a liqueur such as Kahlúa, which is 53 proof or 26.5% ABV

170 calories

0 g protein

0 g fat

24 g carbohydrate

11 g alcohol

LIQUOR OR SPIRIT	RECIPE
Tequila blanco Tequila añejo Tequila reposado	Sauces, mops, marinades
Light rums Dark rums Spiced rums	Soups and stews, meat marinades and sauces, barbecue sauces and mops; enhances bold cooking. Pairs great with chocolate and other desserts. Often can be used as substitute for vanilla extract if the desire is a more unique flavor.
Gin	Lighter fare such as desserts, dishes with berries or greens, and as a dressing and light sauce
Vodka and flavored vodkas	Sauces for pasta and poultry; when flavored with herbs and botanicals, great for sauces
Coffee- and nut-flavored liqueurs	Desserts, including cakes, pies, chocolates; some savory sauces; and marinades for meats and poultry, including game meats, pork, and lamb
Fruit- and floral-flavored liqueurs	Desserts and sweet dishes, and dessert sauces
Whiskey, scotch, and bourbon	Savory sauces and marinades, when a stronger, more robust flavor is desired. Great with smoked meats and smoke-infused marinades.
Brandies and cognac	Sauces both savory and sweet; desserts, including chocolate truffles; excellent as a finishing flavor to shellfish soups and bisques

Guide to Liquors & Spirits

This guide to popular liquors and spirits lists each one's color, flavor, source, alcohol content (by volume), and possible substitutes. Use this chart with the recipes in this book, or let it help you dream up new, delicious drinks!

SPIRIT	COLOR	FLAVOR
Absinthe	green	herbal, licorice
Amaretto	amber	sweet almond, spice
Anisette	clear	licorice
Apple brandy	amber	apple, oak
Armagnac	amber	subtle fruit, floral, oak
Benedictine	amber	sweet herb, citrus, slightly bitter medicinal
Benedictine and brandy (B and B)	amber	spicy herb, orange
Bitters	dark	herbal, pepper, slightly medicinal
Brandy	amber	grape, caramel, oak, subtle smoke
Calvados	amber	apple, caramel, vanilla
Campari	red	sweet and tart, herbs, orange
Chambord	purple	blackberry
Chartreuse	green / yellow	bitter herb, cloves, botanical
Chocolate liqueur	white / dark	chocolate, cream, cocoa
Coffee liqueur	amber	coffee, vanilla
Cognac	white / dark	ripe fruit, caramel, oak
Cointreau	red	bittersweet, tangy, orange
Crème de banana	white / green	sweet banana, spice
Crème de cacao	amber	sweet/dark cocoa, cream
Crème de cassis	amber	black currant, jam
Crème de menthe	white / dark	spearmint
Drambuie	red	sweet herbs, smoky scotch, honey

SOURCE	ALCOHOL CONTENT	SUBSTITUTE
wormwood, herbs	70%	Anisette, Pernod
alcohol, sugar, apricot	28%	Add almond extract to brandy.
anise	25 to 40%	Pernod, Sambuca, Ouzo, Absinthe
brandy, apples	20%	Calvados
white wine	40%	Brandy, cognac
brandy	40%	none
brandy	39%	Combine equal parts Benedictine with brandy and orange liqueur.
roots, herbs	40%	none
white wine	35 to 45%	Armagnac, cognac
brandy, apple	40%	Add apple cider to brandy.
alcohol, herbs, spices, fruit peel	24.7%	none
cognac, raspberry, herbs	23%	Framboise
wine, herbs and botanicals	55%	none
alcohol, chocolate	12 to 24%	Mix chocolate syrup with Irish cream.
alcohol, coffee	20%	Kahlua, Tia Maria
white grapes	40%	Armagnac, brandy
brandy, orange peel	40%	Triple Sec, Grand Marnier
alcohol, bananas	15 to 23%	Brandy and banana extract
alcohol, chocolate	15 to 24%	Chocolate cream liqueur
alcohol, black currants	18 to 25%	Chambord
mint	15%	Peppermint schnapps
scotch, honey	40%	Honey liqueur

SPIRIT	COLOR	FLAVOR
Framboise (raspberry liqueur)	purple	sweet, sugar, raspberry
Frangelico	dark	hazelnut, cocoa, vanilla, toast
Gin	clear	juniper berry, citrus, floral, herbal, botanical
Goldschlager	clear / gold	spicy, cinnamon, syrup
Grand Marnier	amber	sweet orange
Irish cream liqueur (Bailey's)	cream	sweet nutty, spicy
Irish Mist	amber	whiskey, herbs, floral
Kirsch brandy	amber	cherries
Limoncello di Leva	yellow	sweet lemon
Melon liqueur (Midori)	green	honeydew melon
Ouzo	clear	spicy licorice
Peach schnapps	clear	ripe peach
Pear liqueur	clear	ripe pears
Pernod	clear	licorice
Rum, coconut	clear	sweet vanilla
Rum, dark	dark	molasses, vanilla
Rum, white	clear	sugar, orange
Sambuca	clear	licorice, anise
Southern Comfort	amber	peach, whiskey
Tequila, Agave	clear	herb, pepper, hint of citrus
Tequila, Anjeo	amber	herb, smoke, wood, pepper
Tequila, Reposado	amber	herb, smoke, oak
Triple Sec	clear	tart orange
Vodka	clear	very subtle herb, alcohol
Whiskey, American	amber / dark	caramel, smoke, spice
Whisky, Canadian	amber / dark	vanilla, caramel, smoke
Whiskey, Irish	amber / dark	smoke, fruit, creamy butter
Whisky, Scotch	amber / dark	caramel, herbs, spice, smoke
Yukon Jack	amber	orange, whisky

SOURCE	ALCOHOL CONTENT	SUBSTITUTE
raspberries	16%	Chambord
hazelnuts	24%	Walnut liqueur
juniper berries, wheat or rye	40%	none
cinnamon	40%	Cinnamon schnapps
cognac, oranges	42%	Cointreau, Triple Sec
Irish whiskey, cream	17%	none
whiskey, herbs	35%	none
cherries	37 to 45%	Cherry whiskey, cherry
lemons	30 to 35%	Lemon-flavored vodka
melon	15 to 24%	none
grapes, anise, cloves	40%	Anisette, Pernod
peaches	15 to 25%	Apricot brandy
pears	30%	Poire au Cognac
anise	40%	Sambuca, Anisette, Ouzo
sugar cane, coconut	20 to 35%	Rum with coconut extract
sugar cane	40 to 80%	White rum
sugar cane, orange	35%	none
witch elder bush, herbs, spices	38%	Ouzo, Anisette
whiskey, fruit	35%	Whiskey with peach juice
blue agave	40 to 50%	none
blue agave	40 to 50%	none
blue agave	40 to 50%	none
orange rind	22 to 35%	Cointreau, Grand Marnier
grain, corn, potato, grapes	40 to 50%	none
corn and grain	40 to 75%	Scotch, rye
rye	40%	Bourbon, scotch
barley, wheat or corn	40%	Bourbon, rye, scotch
barley, wheat or corn	40 to 75%	Bourbon, rye
whisky and orange rind	40%	Orange brandy

Sauces, Marinades, Dressings, and More

Tequila Lime Vinaigrette

Hundreds of store-bought salad dressings and marinades claim to be the freshest, most flavorful, and best. Truthfully, nothing is as fresh or flavorful as what you've made yourself. Lime zest, fresh cilantro, and tequila come together to make this vinaigrette quick, simple, and delicious as either a marinade or a salad dressing.

- 1 teaspoon grated lime zest
- 1/2 teaspoon ground coriander
- 1/4 cup (60 ml) fresh lime juice
- 2 tablespoons (30 ml) tequila
- 2 shallots, minced
- 2 scallions, green and whites parts, minced
- 1 tablespoon (7 g) minced fresh cilantro
- 3/4 cup (175 ml) vegetable oil
  Salt and freshly ground black pepper

In a bowl, combine the lime zest, coriander, lime juice, tequila, shallots, scallions, and cilantro with a whisk. Gradually, in a steady stream, add the vegetable oil while whisking to emulsify. Season with salt and pepper to taste and refrigerate for at least 30 minutes before using as a salad dressing. If using as a marinade, use immediately. Alternatively, if you have a plastic beverage container with a tight-fitting lid, place all the ingredients in the container, cover, and shake vigorously until emulsified.

Prep = 10 minutes **Chill** = 30 minutes for a salad dressing
Yield = 1 1/2 cups (355 ml)

Brandied Peach Preserves

Because of the long cooking time, there is virtually no alcohol aftertaste in the finished preserves, just the rich, deep flavors of wood-aged brandy and sweet peaches. If you can, choose a good-quality brandy with years of aging in oak barrels. This will give the preserves added, remarkable flavor.

6	pounds (2.75 k, or about 20) fresh peaches, peeled, pitted, and chopped coarsely, or 5 pounds (2.3 kg) frozen peaches, coarsely chopped
8	cups (1.6 k) granulated sugar
2	sticks cinnamon
1	teaspoon ground nutmeg
2	tablespoons (20 g) whole juniper berries
2	teaspoons whole cloves
1	teaspoon ground allspice
	Zest from 1 lemon, or 2 sprigs fresh lemon verbena
2	cups (475 ml) brandy
1	tablespoon (15 ml) peach schnapps
1/2	cup (120 ml) gin

Prepare a large pot filled with enough water to cover one dozen 1/2-pint (240 ml) jars by 2 inches (5 cm). Bring the water to a boil. Sterilize your jars and lids in the boiling water for 5 minutes. Remove and dry. Meanwhile, combine all the ingredients in a saucepan over medium-high heat. Bring the liquid to a boil, stirring occasionally. Lower the heat and simmer until the peaches have become transparent, about 1 1/2 hours. Transfer the jam to the sterilized jars. Wipe the jars clean and secure the lids. Place in the pot of boiling water and boil for 5 minutes. Transfer to a cooling rack to let cool completely. Store the jars in a cool, dry place. Once opened, store in the refrigerator.

Prep = 15 minutes **Cook** = 1 1/2 hours
Yield = about 1 dozen 1/2-pint (240 ml) jars

Amaretto Honey Butter

A trick of the restaurant trade is compound or flavored butters. Whether used as a finish to a sauce, a spread for warm breads, or a topping to a grilled steak, flavored butters add a subtle finished flavor to any dish. This butter is sweetened with honey and the amaretto adds a tang.

8   tablespoons (1 stick, or 112 g) unsalted butter, softened
1   teaspoon honey
1   teaspoon amaretto liqueur

Place the butter in a small bowl, add the honey and liqueur, and mash together using a fork. Scrape the butter onto a piece of plastic warp, forming it into a log shape. Wrap the butter log in the plastic wrap and refrigerate until ready to use. Slice pieces of butter for scones or bread, or use on top of grilled meats and fish. Keep wrapped and refrigerated.

Prep = 5 minutes   **Chill** = 30 minutes   **Yield** = 8 tablespoons (112 g)

Spicy Peach BBQ Sauce

Barbecue sauce and peaches are hallmarks of Southern-style cuisine, but rarely are they together in one recipe. With peach schnapps, this sweet, robust sauce will spice up pork, meat, and chicken. If peach schnapps is not available, try orange liqueur.

- 2 tablespoons (30 ml) extra-virgin olive oil
- 1 medium yellow onion, minced
- 1 large peach, peeled, pitted, and finely chopped
- 2 cloves garlic, minced
- ¼ cup (60 ml) brandy
- ¼ cup (60 ml) peach schnapps
- 1½ cups (360 g) ketchup
- 2 tablespoons (30 ml) Worcestershire sauce
- 2 tablespoons (30 ml) cider vinegar
- 1 teaspoon dry mustard
- 1 tablespoon (9 g) chili powder
- ½ teaspoon salt
- ½ cup (112 g) tomato sauce
- 1 tablespoon (7 g) packed dark brown sugar

In a saucepan, heat the olive oil over medium-high heat. Add the onion and sauté until just tender. Add the peach and garlic and cook, stirring, for 2 minutes. Add the brandy and schnapps and cook for 2 minutes. Stir in the ketchup, Worcestershire sauce, cider vinegar, mustard, chili powder, salt, tomato sauce, and brown sugar. Lower the heat to a simmer and cook for 20 minutes. Remove from the heat and let cool. If not using immediately, transfer to a container or jars with tight-fitting lids. Refrigerate until ready to use.

Prep = 20 minutes **Cook** = 30 minutes **Yield** = about 3 cups (710 g)

Whiskey Mustard Mop

Whether in your glass or in your sauce, whiskey is a great grilling companion. This sauce is a delicious blend of grainy mustard, sweet honey, and robust whiskey. Use as a marinade or a barbecue mop for grilling. It's great on chicken and pulled pork any time of the year.

2 tablespoons (30 ml) olive or vegetable oil
½ cup (65 g) chopped sweet yellow onion
¼ cup (60 ml) sour mash whiskey, such as Jack Daniels
1 cup (235 g) coarse-grained mustard
1 cup (225 g) mayonnaise
2 tablespoons (40 g) honey
2 tablespoons (13 g) packed light brown sugar
Pinch of ground cloves

In a small saucepan, heat the olive oil over medium heat. Add the onion and sauté until just tender and beginning to turn golden, about 3 minutes. Add the whiskey and cook for 1 minute. Remove from the heat and stir in the mustard, mayonnaise, honey, brown sugar, and cloves. Let cool. Store in an airtight container, refrigerated, for up to 2 weeks.

Prep = 10 minutes **Cook** = 6 minutes **Yield** = about 3 cups (710 g)

Sauce Bordelaise

Sauce Bordelaise is a classic French sauce that marries Sauce Espagnole, or brown sauce, with red wine. It originated in the Bordeaux region of France, and using dry, red Bordeaux in the classic preparation. Here, I use red wine but blend it with an equal amount of brandy giving the sauce a more elegant, velvety flavor.

- ¼ cup (55 g) butter
- ½ cup (80 g) minced shallot
- 1 clove garlic, crushed
- ¼ cup (32 g) all-purpose flour
- 1 (10½ ounce, [315 ml]) can condensed beef broth
- ¼ cup (60 ml) dry red wine
- ¼ cup (60 ml) brandy
- 1 tablespoon (4 g) minced fresh flat-leaf parsley
- ¼ teaspoon dried thyme
- 1 dry bay leaf
- ¼ teaspoon salt
- ½ teaspoon Worcestershire sauce

Melt the butter in a medium saucepan over medium-high heat. Add the shallots and garlic and sauté until the shallots are transparent, about 3 minutes. Sprinkle in the flour and continue to cook, stirring constantly, until the flour is a rich, golden brown. Using a whisk, slowly add the beef broth, stirring constantly. Add the wine and brandy, stirring constantly until thickened. Stir in the parsley, thyme, bay leaf, salt, and Worcestershire sauce. Continue cooking and stirring until the sauce comes to a boil and is thickened. Discard the bay leaf and serve over your favorite grilled steak.

Prep = 10 minutes **Cook** = 15 minutes **Yield** = about 2 cups (470 ml)

Honey Lime
Dipping Sauce

This dipping sauce is perfect for chips, cut vegetables, crostini, or the delicious Margarita Chicken Wings on page 114. Make this sauce ahead of time, giving it plenty of time in the refrigerator for the flavors to come together. Since it calls for such a small amount, use good-quality, well-aged añejo tequila.

1   cup (230 g) light sour cream
1   teaspoon añejo or lime-flavored tequila
2   tablespoons (28 g) olive oil-based mayonnaise
1   teaspoon lime zest
     Juice of 2 limes
6   drops hot sauce
1   teaspoon ground cumin
1   tablespoon (20 g) honey
4   scallions, green and white parts, finely chopped
     Freshly ground sea salt

Combine all the ingredients in a small bowl, seasoning with salt to taste, and stir. Cover with plastic wrap and refrigerate for at least 2 hours and up to overnight. Made ahead, the dipping sauce can be stored in an airtight container in the refrigerator for 5 days.

Prep = 15 minutes   **Chill** = at least 2 hours   **Yield** =1$\frac{1}{2}$ cups (355 g)

Bourbon Black Pepper BBQ Sauce

This sweet, spicy sauce obtains its oomph from dry mustard, a hearty dose of pepper, and an entire cup of bourbon—not for the faint-hearted!

3   tablespoons (45 ml) extra-virgin olive oil
1   medium sweet yellow onion, diced
1   jalapeño pepper, seeded and minced
4   cloves garlic, minced
1   cup (235 ml) bourbon
2   cups (475 g) ketchup
1/3 cup (80 ml) Worcestershire sauce
2   tablespoons (40 g) molasses
1/4 cup (55 g) packed dark brown sugar
1   tablespoon (7 g) dry mustard
1   tablespoon (6 g) freshly cracked black pepper
1/2 teaspoon freshly ground sea salt

Heat the olive oil in a saucepan over medium heat. Add the onion, jalapeño, and garlic and sauté until the onion just turns translucent, about 7 minutes. Add the bourbon and cook, stirring, for 3 minutes. Add the ketchup, Worcestershire sauce, molasses, brown sugar, dry mustard, black pepper, and salt, stir to combine, and cook for 20 minutes, until thickened. Store in an airtight container, refrigerated, for up to 4 weeks.

Prep = 10 minutes **Cook** = 30 minutes **Yield** = about 3 cups (710 g)

Vanilla Vodka, Cherry-Apricot Chutney

Chutney is a versatile condiment to have on hand. Refrigerated, chutney lasts for at least two weeks. Prepare this ahead and refrigerate until ready to use as a topping on grilled fish, poultry, or pork, or as a spread on your favorite toasted breads and scones.

- 1 tablespoon (15 ml) vegetable oil
- 1 cup (130 g) chopped sweet yellow onion
- 1 tablespoon (6 g) minced fresh ginger
- 1/4 cup (60 ml) vanilla-flavored vodka
- 1 tablespoon (5 g) mustard seeds
- 1 teaspoon curry powder
- 1/8 teaspoon ground nutmeg
- 1/4 teaspoon ground cinnamon
- 1/2 pound (225 g) dried apricots, chopped
- 1/2 pound (225 g) dried cherries, chopped
- 3/4 cup (120 g) golden raisins
- 1/4 cup (40 g) currants
- 1/2 cup (120 ml) cider vinegar
- 1/2 cup (100 g) granulated sugar
- 1/2 teaspoon coarse sea salt
- 1/2 teaspoon black pepper

Heat the oil in a medium skillet over medium-high heat. Sauté the onion and ginger until lightly browned, about 5 minutes. Add the vodka, mustard seeds, curry powder, nutmeg, and cinnamon. Stirring constantly, cook for 3 minutes. Add the apricots, cherries, raisins, currants, cider vinegar, and sugar, stirring to combine. Lower the heat to a simmer and cook for about 10 minutes, until the liquid has reduced and the chutney is thick. Remove from the heat, season with salt and black pepper, and let cool.

Prep = 10 minutes **Cook** = 18 minutes **Yield** = 4 cups (1 k)

Smoked Bourbon BBQ Sauce

A good barbecue sauce is a kitchen staple year-round. As a condiment, dipping sauce, or smear for grilling, it's a foolproof way to add bold flavor to many dishes. Use this sauce for grilled meats and chicken and as basting sauce for the Chicken on a Bottle (page 103).

2 tablespoons (30 ml) rendered bacon fat or vegetable oil
1/2 cup (65 g) minced sweet yellow onion
1 clove fresh garlic, minced
1 cup (235 g) ketchup
1/3 cup (80 ml) bourbon
2 tablespoons (40 g) molasses
1 tablespoon (20 g) honey
2 tablespoons (13 g) packed dark brown sugar
1 teaspoon liquid smoke
2 tablespoons (30 ml) Worcestershire sauce
1 teaspoon dry mustard

Heat the bacon fat in a small saucepan over medium-high heat. Add the onion and garlic and sauté for 1 minute, just until tender. Add the ketchup, bourbon, molasses, honey, brown sugar, liquid smoke, Worcestershire sauce, and dry mustard, and simmer for 10 minutes over low heat. Remove from the heat and allow to cool completely. Store in an airtight jar in the refrigerator until ready to use. Will keep for 2 weeks.

Prep = 10 minutes **Cook** = 12 minutes **Yield** = about 2 cups (475 g)

Fruit and Spirit Syrups

(Adapted from *Small Batch Preserving*
by Ellie Topp and Margaret Howard)

Fruit syrups are simple and versatile; the basic syrup recipe can be used in several applications. Salad, desserts, drinks, and savory dishes alike come alive with these syrups. Cherry and Amaretto Syrup is delicious over cakes and ice cream; Pear Syrup with Brandy is an excellent topping for pound cake and spiced cake as well as for pan-fried pork chops.

Cherry and Amaretto Syrup

Zest and juice of 1 lemon
2 ½ cups (570 ml) water
2 cups (400 g) granulated sugar
7 cups (1.4 k) sweet cherries, pitted
¼ cup (60 ml) amaretto liqueur

Prepare a large pot filled with enough water to cover four 1-pint (475 ml) jars by 2 inches (5 cm). Bring the water to a boil. Sterilize your jars and lids in the boiling water for 5 minutes. Remove and dry. Meanwhile, combine the lemon zest and juice, the 2½ cups (570 ml) water, and the sugar in a large saucepan over high heat. Bring to a boil and boil for 1 minute. Place 1 tablespoon (15 ml) of the amaretto in each pint jar. Pack the jars with as many cherries as will fill the jars to the rim. Add the syrup to the jars to just cover the cherries. Remove any air bubbles by running the handle of a wooden spoon between the fruit and the glass. Wipe the jars clean and secure the lids. Place in the pot of boiling water and boil for 15 minutes. Transfer to a cooling rack to let cool completely. Store the jars in a cool, dry place. Once opened, store in the refrigerator.

Prep = 10 minutes **Cook** = 15 minutes
Yield = about 4 (1-pint [475 ml]) jars

Pear Syrup with Brandy

Zest and juice of 1 lemon
2 ½ cups (570 ml) water
2 cups (400 g) granulated sugar
6 tablespoons (90 ml) brandy
3 sticks cinnamon
6 cups (1.2 kg) ripe, peeled, cored and sliced pears

Prepare a large pot filled with enough water to cover three 1-pint (475 ml) jars by 2 inches (5 cm). Bring the water to a boil. Sterilize the jars and lids in the boiling water for 5 minutes. Remove and dry. Meanwhile, combine the lemon zest and juice, the 2 ½ cups (570 ml) water, and the sugar in a large saucepan over high heat. Bring to a boil and boil for 1 minute. Place 2 tablespoons (30 ml) of the brandy and 1 cinnamon stick in each pint jar. Pack the jars with as many pears as will fill the jars to the rim. Add the syrup to the jars to just cover the fruit. Remove any air bubbles by running the handle of a wooden spoon between the fruit and the glass. Wipe the jars clean and secure the lids. Place in the pot of boiling water and boil for 20 minutes. Transfer to a cooling rack to let cool completely. Store the jars in a cool, dry place. Once opened, store in the refrigerator.

Prep = 20 minutes **Cook** = 20 minutes
Yield = 3 (1-pint [475 ml]) jars

Cranberry Rum Relish

(Adapted from *Small Batch Preserving*
by Ellie Topp and Margaret Howard)

Dark rum and its spiced character and hints of
caramel and smoke adds a wonderful flavor profile to
this homemade cranberry relish. Gin's herbal, botanical nature complements the tart berries. This relish
is a great condiment for any time of year.

½	cup (120 ml) dark rum
¼	cup (60 ml) gin
¼	cup (35 g) finely chopped shallot
	Grated zest of 1 orange
3 ½	cups (385 g) fresh or frozen cranberries
1 ½	cups (300 g) granulated sugar
1	sprig fresh rosemary
1	teaspoon freshly ground black pepper

Prepare a large pot filled with enough water to cover four ½-pint
(240 ml) jars by 2 inches (5 cm). Bring the water to a boil. Sterilize
your jars and lids in the boiling water for 5 minutes. Remove and
dry. Meanwhile, combine the rum, gin, shallots, and orange zest in
a saucepan over high heat. Bring to a boil, lower the heat to a simmer, and cook until the mixture has reduced to a syrupy consistency,
about 10 minutes. Add the cranberries, sugar, and rosemary. Cook
until the cranberries have popped and the sugar has dissolved.
Remove from the heat and stir in the ground pepper. Remove the
rosemary sprig. Ladle into the sterilized jars. Wipe the jars clean and
secure the lids. Place in the pot of boiling water and boil for 10 minutes. Transfer to a cooling rack to let cool completely. Store the jars
in a cool, dry place. Once opened, store in the refrigerator.

Prep = 10 minutes **Cook** = about 30 minutes
Yield =4 (½-pint [240 ml]) jars

Plum Amaretto Jam

Almonds are typically considered complementary to cherries. Plums, just a branch away on the *Prunus* family tree, create a delightful variation on this traditional combination.

- 4 cups (1 k) seeded and chopped red or purple plums
- 4 cups (800 g) granulated sugar
- 1/3 cup (80 ml) water
- 1/4 cup (60 ml) freshly squeezed lemon juice
- 1/2 cup (120 ml) amaretto liqueur

Prepare a large pot filled with enough water to cover eight 1/2-pint (240 ml) jars by 2 inches (5 cm). Bring the water to a boil. Sterilize your jars and lids in the boiling water for 5 minutes. Remove and dry. Meanwhile, combine the plums, sugar, the 1/3 cup (80 ml) of water, and the lemon juice in a large saucepan over high heat. Bring to a boil, lower the heat to medium, and boil for 20 minutes, stirring frequently. Remove from the heat and stir in the amaretto. Ladle the jam into the sterilized jars and boil in a pot of boiling water for 5 minutes. Transfer the jars to a cooling rack to cool completely. Transfer to a cooling rack to let cool completely. Store the jars in a cool, dry place. Once opened, store in the refrigerator.

Prep = 10 minutes **Cook** = 30 minutes
Yield = 8 (1/2-pint [240 ml]) jars

Raspberry Kirsch Jam

Kirschwasser, or Kirsch, is a flavored brandy made from the pits and meat of Morello cherries. Unlike some cherry liqueurs that are overly sweet, Kirsch is subtler, with an almond undertone from the pits. Here, use raspberries with a cherry brandy instead of a raspberry liqueur—the natural sugars add natural sweetness.

- 2 pounds (910 g) fresh raspberries
- 1 Bosc pear, peeled, cored, and finely chopped
- 1/4 cup (60 ml) fresh lemon juice
- 1/2 cup (120 ml) still mineral water
- 3/4 cup (150 g) granulated sugar
- 1/4 cup (60 ml) Kirsch

Prepare a large pot filled with enough water to cover four 1/2-pint (240 ml) jars by 2 inches (5 cm). Bring the water to a boil. Sterilize your jars and lids in the boiling water for 5 minutes. Remove and dry. Combine the raspberries, pear, lemon juice, and mineral water in a saucepan over medium heat. Simmer for 30 minutes. Add the sugar and bring to a boil, stirring constantly. Lower the heat and simmer for 1 hour, until thickened. Remove from the heat, stir in the Kirsch, and let stand for 5 minutes. Ladle into the sterilized jars. Wipe the jars clean and secure the lids. Place in the pot of boiling water and boil for 10 minutes. Transfer to a cooling rack to let cool completely. Store the jars in a cool, dry place. Once opened, store in the refrigerator. Will keep, sealed, for one year.

Prep = 10 minutes **Cook** = 1 1/2 hours
Yield = 4 (1/2-pint [240 ml]) jars

Dijon Whiskey Sauce

Yet another pairing of mustard and whiskey, this recipe is augmented by a dash of hot pepper sauce.

 1/4 cup (60 ml) extra-virgin olive or vegetable oil
 3 sweet yellow onions, chopped
 2 tablespoons (12 g) peeled and chopped fresh ginger
 1 tablespoon (14 g) tomato paste
 1/2 cup (120 ml) whiskey
 2 cups (470 g) tomato purée
 3/4 cup (175 ml) dark molasses
 1/4 cup (60 g) coarse-grained Dijon mustard
 1/2 cup (120 ml) cider vinegar
 1/3 cup (80 ml) Worcestershire sauce
 1/2 teaspoon freshly ground sea salt
 1 teaspoon freshly ground black pepper
 1 teaspoon hot pepper sauce
 2 tablespoons (40 g) honey

Heat the oil in a large saucepan over medium heat. Add the onion and sauté for 3 minutes. Add the ginger and sauté for an additional 2 minutes. Add the tomato paste, stirring until well combined and not lumpy. Add the whiskey and cook, stirring, for 3 minutes. Add the tomato purée, molasses, mustard, vinegar, Worcestershire sauce, salt, pepper, hot pepper sauce, and honey and cook, stirring, for 15 minutes. Remove from the heat and let cool completely. Store in an airtight container, refrigerated, for up to 4 weeks.

Prep = 10 minutes **Cook** = 25 minutes
Yield = about 6 cups (1.4 L)

Piña Colada Jam

This jam is almost drinkable. Seldom do you find a good pineapple jam or preserves, though the fruit is excellent in salsas, syrups, and jams. If fresh ripe pineapples are available, do substitute them for canned, weighing the pineapple to get thirty ounces (840 g) of fruit and juice.

- 2 (14½-ounce [412 g]) cans pineapple, chopped
- 5 cups (1 k) granulated sugar
- 1 cup (235 ml) coconut-flavored rum
- 2 cinnamon sticks
- 1 tablespoon (10 g) juniper berries
- 1 teaspoon ground ginger
- 1 tablespoon (15 ml) apple cider vinegar

Prepare a large pot filled with enough water to cover four ½-pint (240 ml) jars by 2 inches (5 cm). Bring the water to a boil. Sterilize your jars and lids in the boiling water for 5 minutes. Remove and dry. Combine all the ingredients in a saucepan over medium-high heat. Bring to a boil, lower the heat, and cook for 2 hours, until thickened. Ladle into the sterilized jars. Wipe the jars clean and secure the lids. Place in the pot of boiling water and boil for 5 minutes. Transfer to a cooling rack to let cool completely. Store the jars in a cool, dry place. Once opened, store in the refrigerator.

Prep = 20 minutes **Cook** = 2 hours
Yield = 4 (½-pint [240 ml]) jars

Infused Vodkas

Flavored liquors and spirits are as popular as ever, but the store-bought versions are often made with artificial syrups and flavorings with no real fruit or herbs added. Making your own at home is very simple and rewarding because the flavors are fresh. Use the basic techniques below for any combination of flavors. Set these aside for your favorite drinks, for the recipes in this book, or to give as gifts.

Chili Pepper Vodka (opposite, left)

    4   whole hot peppers (jalapeño, habanero, red Thai, or anaheim)
    2   cups (475 ml) premium vodka

Wash and thoroughly dry the peppers. Slice the peppers in half (for a mild pepper vodka, remove the veins and seeds). Place the peppers and vodka in a jar or bottle with a tight-fitting lid and store in a dry, cool place for 5 days. Strain the vodka through a fine-mesh sieve into a bottle with a tight-fitting lid. Store until ready to use.

Berry Vodka (opposite, middle)

    3   pints (900 g) red raspberries
    1   pint (300 g) blueberries
    1   cup (200 g) granulated sugar
    4   cups (950 ml) good-quality vodka

Place the berries in a bowl and mash with a potato masher to extrude their juices. Add the sugar and stir. Scrape the berry mixture into a jar or container with a tight-fitting lid. Add the vodka and shake to combine thoroughly and dissolve the sugar. Store in a cool, dry place for 1 week. Strain the mixture through a fine-mesh sieve into a bottle. (If your strainer is not fine enough, line it with a coffee filter or double layer of paper towels and strain the vodka through one more time into the jar.) Store until ready to use.

Prep = 10 minutes **Rest** = 5 days
Yield = 2 cups (470 ml)

Basil Vodka (above, right)

- 24 large fresh basil leaves
- 4 cups (950 ml) good-quality vodka

Wash and thoroughly dry the basil leaves. Place 6 basil leaves in a bowl with 1 cup (235 ml) of the vodka and use a wooden spoon to bruise the basil leaves while stirring them in the vodka. Place the remaining 3 cups (715 ml) vodka in an airtight container or bottle with a tight-fitting lid. Strain the basil-infused vodka into the container and pack with the remaining basil leaves. Refrigerate for at least 24 hours and up to 2 days. Strain the basil vodka through a fine-mesh sieve into a bottle with a tight-fighting lid. Store in the refrigerator until ready to use.

Prep = 5 minutes **Rest** = 1 to 2 days
Yield = 4 cups (940 ml)

Rosemary Vodka

4 long sprigs fresh rosemary
2 cups (475 ml) good-quality vodka

Wash and thoroughly dry the rosemary sprigs. Place in a bottle with a tight-fitting lid and pour in the vodka. Seal and store for 2 to 3 days. Remove all but one of the rosemary sprigs and store the flavored vodka until when ready to use.

Chamomile Tea Vodka

2 tablespoons (8 g) chamomile tea leaves
2 cups (475 ml) good-quality vodka

Combine the ingredients in a jar with a tight-fitting lid and let sit for 5 days to infuse. When ready to use the vodka in a recipe, strain through a fine-mesh sieve.

Orange Vodka

3 large oranges
4 cups (950 ml) good-quality vodka

Wash and thoroughly dry the oranges. Using a zester or vegetable peeler, peel the zest from the orange, leaving behind as much pith as possible. Trim away any remaining pith and discard. Twist the orange zest pieces, bruising them to release their essence. Place all the zest in a jar with a tight-fitting lid and fill with the vodka. Store in a cool, dry place for up to 1 week. Strain the vodka into a jar through a fine-mesh sieve. Store until ready to use.

Prep = 5 to 10 minutes **Store** = 7 to 10 days **Yield** = 2 to 4 cups

Espresso Vodka

- 1 cup (235 ml) water
- 2 tablespoons (14 g) instant espresso powder
- 1 cup (200 g) granulated sugar
- 2 cups (475 ml) good-quality vodka
- 1 teaspoon pure vanilla extract

Bring the water to a boil in a small saucepan. Add the espresso powder, stirring until it dissolves. Lower the heat to low and add the sugar, stirring until it dissolves;, set aside to cool. Once cool, add the vodka and vanilla; stir to combine. Pour the vodka into jars with tight-fitting lids. Store in a cool, dark place to infuse for at least 48 hours.

Tomato Vine Vodka

- 4 fresh-from-the-garden tomato plant stems with leaves
- 2 cups (475 ml) good-quality vodka

Wash and pat dry the tomato leaves. Place in a jar or bottle and add the vodka. Secure the lid and let infuse for 5 days. Use in favorite cocktails or recipes. For added visual affect, add a couple of whole cherry or grape tomatoes of varying colors to the jar.

Prep = 15 minutes **Store** = 7 to 10 days **Yield** = 4 cups

Breakfast
and Brunch

Spiced Rum Muffins with Cranberries and Pecans

These muffins are a quick, everyday breakfast treat made from packaged gingerbread mix and a few key ingredients. Spiced rum, with its caramel sweetness, pairs perfectly with the ginger and cranberries, making a moist, delicious meal or snack.

1	(14½-ounce [412 g]) package prepared gingerbread cake mix
¼	cup (28 g) all-purpose flour
¼	cup (60 ml) spiced rum
¾	cup (175 ml) milk
2	eggs
1	cup (75 g) rolled oats
1	cup (150 g) dried cranberries
½	cup (62 g) chopped pecans

Preheat the oven to 350°F (180°C, or gas mark 4). Spray a 6-cup muffin tin with nonstick cooking spray. Mix the cake mix together with the flour, rum, milk, and eggs in a bowl just until combine. Add the oats, cranberries, and pecans and mix together just to combine. Spoon the mixture into the muffin tins and bake for 25 minutes, until a toothpick inserted into the center of one muffin comes out clean.

Prep = 10 minutes **Cook** = 25 minutes **Yield** = 6 large muffins

Sweet Bread French Toast with Orange-Peach Compote

Orange liqueur and amaretto are a sweet, flavorful combination, and nothing complements French toast better.

4 eggs
¾ cup (175 ml) whole milk
¼ cup (60 ml) orange liqueur, such as Grand Marnier
1 tablespoon (15 ml) amaretto liqueur
   Pinch of ground cloves
1 tablespoon (13 g) granulated sugar
1 loaf day-old sweet bread
4 to 6 tablespoons (55 to 83 g) butter

ORANGE-PEACH COMPOTE:
16 ounces (455 g) frozen peaches, thawed
¼ cup (50 g) granulated sugar
¼ cup (60 ml) orange liqueur
½ cup (62 g) chopped, toasted pecans
¼ cup (60 ml) maple syrup
¼ teaspoon ground cloves

In a large bowl, whisk the eggs until smooth. Add the milk, orange and amaretto liqueurs, cloves, and sugar. Whisk to combine. Slice the sweet bread into 6 slices, then cut in half. Preheat a large skillet over medium heat and melt 2 tablespoons (28 g) of the butter. Working in batches, probably 3 slices of bread at a time, dip the bread into the batter, coating well. Place in the hot pan and cook until browned on one side, about 4 minutes. Turn and continue to cook until browned, about 4 minutes longer. Transfer to warm plates. Repeat until all the batches are cooked, adding more butter as needed.

For the orange-peach compote: Place all the ingredients in a saucepan over medium-high heat. Bring to a boil. Stirring periodically, boil the mixture until it cooks down and becomes thickened, about 10 minutes. Serve hot over the French toast.

Prep = 10 minutes **Cook** = 12 to 14 minutes per batch
Yield = 4 servings

Baked Pear French Toast

This stuffed French toast comes together quickly and cooks in 30 minutes—it is a true breakfast treat.

- 5 eggs
- 1 cup (235 ml) milk
- 1/2 cup (120 ml) heavy cream
- 1/2 cup (120 ml) Irish cream liqueur
- 1/4 teaspoon ground cinnamon
- 1/4 teaspoon ground nutmeg
- 1/2 teaspoon pure vanilla extract
- 2 tablespoons (25 g) granulated sugar
- 1 large loaf cinnamon swirl brioche or sweet bread, sliced into 12 slices
- 4 tablespoons (1/2 stick, or 55 g) unsalted butter
- 4 Bosc or Bartlett pears, peeled, cored, and thinly sliced
- 1 cup (125 g) chopped walnuts
- 1/2 cup (83 g) golden raisins
- 1/2 cup (120 ml) Poire William or apple brandy
- 1/2 cup (112 g) packed light brown sugar
- 1/2 teaspoon ground cinnamon
- 1/2 teaspoon ground nutmeg
- 2 tablespoons (30 ml) maple syrup

Preheat the oven to 350°F (180°C, or gas mark 4). In a large bowl, whisk the eggs until smooth. Add the milk, heavy cream, Irish cream, cinnamon, nutmeg, vanilla, and granulated sugar, whisking to combine well. Set aside. Spray a 9 × 13-inch (23 × 33 cm) baking pan with nonstick cooking spray. Layer 6 slices of brioche in the pan in a single layer, laying all the slices in the same direction. In a large skillet, melt the butter over medium-high heat, add the pears, raisins, and walnuts, and cook for 4 minutes. Add the Poire William and stir to combine; cook for 2 minutes. Add the brown sugar, cinnamon, nutmeg, and maple syrup, stir to combine, and cook for 4 additional minutes to thicken. Pour the pear mixture in an even layer over the layer of brioche slices in the prepared pan. Layer the remaining 6 brioche slices over the pears, lining up each slice to face the same direction as the one below it. Pour the milk mixture over the bread, coating evenly. Press the bread slightly to soak up the milk mixture and let stand for 5 minutes. Place in the oven and bake until browned and set, about 30 minutes. Cut the bread slices into two layered triangles and serve warm with maple syrup and butter.

Prep = 20 minutes **Cook** = 30 minutes **Yield** = 6 servings

Amaretto Scones with Almonds and Currants

Scones are perfect for making ahead of time and storing for a couple of days. They are excellent toasted and served with jam (especially one from this book!). These scones have a unique amaretto flavor, giving a touch of almond and orange to the dough.

2 1/2 cups (275 g) all-purpose flour
1/3 cup (67 g) granulated sugar
1 tablespoon (4.6 g) baking powder
1/2 teaspoon salt
10 tablespoons (1 stick plus 2 tablespoons, or 140 g) cold unsalted butter, cut into small pieces
2 eggs
1/2 cup (120 ml) heavy cream
Zest of 1 orange
2 tablespoons (30 ml) amaretto liqueur
1/2 cup (62 g) sliced almonds
1/2 cup (83 g) currants or raisins

Preheat the oven to 350ºF (180ºC, or gas mark 4). Spray a sheet pan with nonstick cooking spray. In the bowl of a food processor fitted with the blade attachment, combine the flour, sugar, baking powder, and salt, and pulse to combine. Add the butter and pulse several times, until a coarse, crumbly meal consistency is reached. Transfer the mixture to a mixing bowl. In a small bowl, lightly beat together the eggs, heavy cream, orange zest, and amaretto liqueur. Add the currants and almonds to the dry mixture, stirring to combine. Add the egg mixture and, with a wooden spoon, lightly stir just to combine. Transfer the mixture to a lightly floured work surface and knead a few times, to make a soft, semimoist dough that holds together. Press the dough into an 18-inch (45.7 cm) -diameter circle about 1/2 inch (1.3 cm) thick. Cut the scones into 12 equal wedges, place on the prepared pan, and bake for 15 minutes, until golden on top. Transfer to a cooling rack to let cool for 15 minutes. Serve warm with jam or honey. Scones can be stored in an airtight container in a cool, dry place for 5 days.

Prep = 10 minutes **Cook** = 15 minutes **Yield** = 12 scones

Lemon-Lavender Pound Cake with Limoncello Glaze

A favorite garden herb of mine is lavender. Not only does it have a refreshing scent, but it also has a lovely floral taste that adds unexpected flavor to baked goods. Pairing it with citrus and Limoncello makes this pound cake moist and light with a delightful flavor. If you do not have fresh lavender in your garden (or in a friendly neighbor's garden!), you can find dried culinary lavender flowers in many natural food stores' bulk spice section. You can also substitute fresh rosemary or fennel seeds for the lavender.

1	cup (125 g) sifted all-purpose flour
1/8	teaspoon baking soda
	Pinch of salt
1	teaspoon finely chopped culinary lavender, plus additional for garnish
1 1/4	cups (250 g) superfine sugar
16	tablespoons (2 sticks, or 225 g) unsalted butter
	Zest of 2 lemons
4	eggs
1/2	cup (48 g) ground Marcona almonds
	Juice of 1 lemon
2	tablespoons (30 ml) Limoncello

GLAZE:

1 1/2	cups (180 g) confectioners' sugar
1/4	cup (60 ml) Limoncello

Preheat the oven to 325°F (170°C, or gas mark 3). Place a rack in the bottom third of the oven and grease and flour a loaf pan. Onto waxed paper, sift together the flour, baking soda, and salt, and set aside. In the bowl of a stand mixer fitted with the paddle attachment, combine the lavender, superfine sugar, and butter, beating on medium-high speed until creamy and smooth, about 7 minutes. Add the lemon zest and eggs, one at a time, beating well after each addition. Scrape the sides of the bowl and add half of the flour mixture and half of the almonds, beating to combine well. Add the lemon juice and beat to combine. Add the remaining flour and almonds and beat to combine. Beat in the Limoncello. Scrape the batter into the prepared pan and bake for 50 minutes, or until a skewer inserted into the center comes out clean. Remove from the oven and place on a cooling rack for 10 minutes. Using a sharp knife, loosen the sides of the cake from the pan. Invert the cake onto a dish and allow to cool completely. Place on a serving dish and drizzle with the glaze. Sprinkle the top of the cake with additional lavender.

For the glaze: Combine the confectioners' sugar and Limoncello in a bowl, stirring with a fork until smooth. Add additional Limoncello if you prefer a thinner glaze.

Prep = 15 minutes **Cook** = 50 minutes **Yield** = 12 servings

Applesauce Coffee Cake with Calvados

Apple brandy adds delicate flavor to this coffee cake. The layers of dried cranberries and streusel create a beautiful and colorful presentation when sliced.

STREUSEL TOPPING:

- ³/₄ cup (83 g) all-purpose flour
- ¹/₃ cup (75 g) firmly packed light brown sugar
- ¹/₄ cup (50 g) granulated sugar
- 1 teaspoon ground cinnamon
- 8 tablespoons (1 stick, or 112 g) unsalted butter, cut into pieces
- ¹/₂ cup (62 g) pecan halves
- ¹/₂ cup (38 g) rolled oats

CAKE:

- 1¹/₂ cups (165 g) all-purpose flour
- 1¹/₂ teaspoons baking powder
- ¹/₄ teaspoon salt
- 1 teaspoon ground cardamom
- 1 teaspoon ground cinnamon
- 1¹/₄ pounds ([566 g], about 3) tart cooking apples, such as Braeburn or Granny Smith, peeled, cored, and chopped
- 8 tablespoons (1 stick, or 112 g) unsalted butter
- 2 tablespoons (30 ml) orange liqueur
- 3 tablespoons (45 ml) apple brandy, such as Calvados or Laird's Applejack
- 2 eggs
- 1 cup (200 g) granulated sugar
- ¹/₂ cup (112 g) packed light brown sugar
- ¹/₂ cup (120 g) applesauce
- 1 teaspoon pure vanilla extract
- 1 cup (150 g) dried cranberries, chopped

Preheat the oven to 350°F (180°C, or gas mark 4). Grease a 9-inch (23 cm) round springform pan with nonstick cooking spray.

For the streusel topping: In the bowl of a food processor fitted with the blade attachment, combine the flour, brown sugar, sugar, and cinnamon, pulsing to just combine. Add the butter and pulse until the mixture forms tiny beads, just a couple of pulses. Add the pecans and rolled oats and pulse to chop and combine. Transfer the mixture to a mixing bowl. With your fingers, press the butter a bit more into the streusel, making clumps, then set aside.

For the cake: In a mixing bowl, use a whisk or fork to stir together the flour, baking powder, salt, cardamom, and cinnamon. Add the chopped apples, tossing to evenly coat. In a saucepan over medium heat, melt the butter. Add the orange liqueur, apple brandy, and vanilla, stirring to combine, then remove from the heat. In a mixing bowl, use a whisk to beat together the eggs and sugars until smooth and creamy. Add the applesauce and the melted butter mixture, whisking to combine well. Add the apple mixture to the wet ingredients. Using a wooden spoon, gently stir just to combine, until there are no more flour spots or clumps. Spoon half the batter into the prepared pan. Top with the dried cranberries and one-third of the streusel topping. Spoon in the remainder of the batter, smoothing to make an even layer. Top with the remaining streusel topping. Place the pan on a sheet pan to catch any possible drippings. Place on the middle rack of the oven and bake for 70 to 80 minutes, until the streusel is browned and a skewer inserted into the center comes out clean. Transfer to a cooling rack to cool for 15 minutes. Remove the sides of the pan and serve warm.

Prep = 20 minutes **Cook** = 70 to 80 minutes **Yield** = 10 servings

Limoncello and Poppy Seed Muffins

The Italian spirit Limoncello gives a rich and balanced taste to these delicious, moist muffins. Update your classic recipe and make these a new breakfast or brunch favorite.

1 ³/₄ cups (193 g) all-purpose flour
1 tablespoon (4.6 g) baking powder
¹/₂ teaspoon salt
1 cup (200 g) plus 2 tablespoons (25 g) granulated sugar
1 tablespoon (8 g) black poppy seeds
1 large egg
¹/₄ cup (60 ml) milk
¹/₄ cup (60 ml) heavy cream
¹/₄ cup (60 ml) Limoncello liqueur
1 teaspoon finely grated lemon zest
2 tablespoons (30 ml) fresh lemon juice
8 tablespoons (1 stick, or 112 g) unsalted butter, melted and cooled

Preheat the oven to 350°F (180°C, or gas mark 4). Grease and flour the cups of a standard 12-cup muffin tin or a large 6-cup muffin tin. In a bowl, whisk together the flour, baking powder, salt, 1 cup (200 g) of the sugar, and the poppy seeds and set aside. In another bowl, whisk together the egg, milk, cream, Limoncello, lemon zest, and lemon juice. Once the melted butter has cooled, gradually whisk into the milk mixture. Make a well in the center of the dry ingredients. Pour in the milk mixture, stirring with a wooden spoon to just combine, being careful not to overmix. Spoon the batter into the prepared pan and sprinkle each muffin equally with the remaining 2 tablespoons (25 g) sugar. Place the muffin tin on a sheet pan to catch any possible drippings. Place on the middle rack of the oven and bake until a toothpick inserted into the center of one muffin comes out clean, 35 minutes. Transfer to a cooling rack and let cool for 20 minutes. Gently remove the muffins from the tin and serve.

Prep = 15 minutes **Bake** = 35 minutes
Yield = 12 regular or 6 large muffins

Blueberry Oatmeal Pancakes with Amaretto Syrup

Every weekend morning gives you another chance to create a delicious treat. Bursting with fresh blueberries and flavored with rolled oats, these pancakes are rich and hearty.

1 ½ cups (165 g) all-purpose flour, sifted
½ cup (55 g) whole wheat flour
3 tablespoons (38 g) granulated sugar
2 teaspoons baking powder
1 teaspoon baking soda
¼ teaspoon ground nutmeg
1 teaspoon salt
2 eggs, lightly beaten
2 ¼ cups (535 ml) buttermilk
4 tablespoons (½ stick, or 55 g) unsalted butter, melted
½ teaspoon pure vanilla extract
½ teaspoon orange extract or liqueur
1 cup (175 g) cooked rolled oats, cooled
½ cup (55 g) fresh blueberries
Butter and vegetable oil, for cooking

AMARETTO SYRUP:
1 cup (235 ml) pure maple syrup
1 tablespoon (15 ml) amaretto liqueur
¼ cup chopped toasted hazelnuts

In a large mixing bowl, whisk together the flours, sugar, baking powder, baking soda, nutmeg, and salt. In a separate bowl, beat the eggs with the buttermilk to combine. Pour the buttermilk mixture into the dry ingredients, add the melted butter, and, using a whisk, stir to combine. Add the vanilla, orange extract, oatmeal, and blueberries, stirring to just combine. Working in batches, melt 1 tablespoon (14 g) of additional butter with 1 tablespoon (15 ml) of vegetable oil in a large, nonstick pan over medium heat. Pour ½-cup (120 ml) portions of batter into the pan to make pancakes. Cook for 4 minutes, then when little pockets of air begin to form all over the batter of the pancake, it is time to flip, turn, and cook for an additional 3 minutes, until cooked through. Continue cooking all the pancakes, adding butter and oil to the pan as necessary. When using butter, it may be necessary to wipe down the pan a couple of times between batches, as the butter fat may begin to burn in the pan. Serve the pancakes warm with the amaretto syrup and softened butter.

For the amaretto syrup: In a small saucepan, heat the maple syrup with the amaretto and hazelnuts over low heat for 10 minutes. Serve warm.

Prep = 15 minutes **Cook** = 20 minutes
Yield = 4 servings (about 4 pancakes each)

Applesauce Coffee Cake

My friend Kathy makes the best homemade apple-sauce. This coffee cake is inspired by her. Adding apple brandy and orange liqueur takes this moist cake steps above average.

STREUSEL TOPPING:

- ³/₄ cup (83 g) all-purpose flour
- ¹/₃ cup (75 g) firmly packed light brown sugar
- ¹/₄ cup (50 g) granulated sugar
- 1 teaspoon ground cinnamon
- 8 tablespoons (1 stick, or 112 g) unsalted butter
- ¹/₂ cup (38 g) rolled oats
- ¹/₂ cup (62 g) pecans

CAKE:

- 1 ¹/₂ cups (165 g) all-purpose flour
- 1 ¹/₂ teaspoons baking powder
- ¹/₄ teaspoon salt
- 1 teaspoon ground cardamom
- 1 teaspoon ground cinnamon
- 1 pound (455 g) tart cooking apples, such as Braeburn, peeled, cored, and chopped
- 8 tablespoons (1 stick, or 112 g) unsalted butter, melted
- ¹/₂ cup (112 g) packed light brown sugar
- 1 cup (200 g) granulated sugar
- 2 tablespoons (30 ml) orange liqueur, such as Grand Marnier
- 2 tablespoons (30 ml) apple brandy, such as Calvados or Laird's Applejack
- 1 teaspoon pure vanilla extract
- ¹/₂ cup (120 g) applesauce
- 2 eggs
- 1 cup (150 g) dried cranberries

Preheat the oven to 350°F (180°C, or gas mark 4). Spray a nonstick 9-inch (23 cm) round springform pan with nonstick cooking spray.

For the streusel topping: In the bowl of a food processor fitted with the blade attachment, combine the flour, sugars, cinnamon, rolled oats, and pecans. Pulse a couple of times to combine. Add the butter and pulse a few times until a coarse, crumbly texture forms. Transfer the mixture to a bowl and, with your fingers, crumble any large clumps apart. Set aside.

For the cake: In a bowl, whisk together the flour, baking powder, salt, cardamom, and cinnamon. Add the apples and stir to evenly coat; set aside. In another bowl, combine the melted butter with the sugars, orange liqueur, apple brandy, and vanilla, whisking until smooth and creamy. Add the applesauce, stirring to combine. Add the eggs one at a time, beating well after each addition. Pour the wet ingredients into the apples, stirring to just combine, until no more flour streaks are seen; do not overmix. Spoon half the mixture into the prepared pan. Sprinkle the dried cranberries evenly over the top and then sprinkle one-third of the streusel mixture evenly over the cranberries. Spoon in the remainder of the batter, smoothing to make an even layer. Top with the remaining streusel topping. Place the pan on a sheet pan to catch any possible drippings. Bake on the center rack of the oven for 1 hour, until a toothpick inserted into the center comes out clean. Transfer to a cooling rack and let cool for 20 minutes. Remove the sides of the pan and let cool for an additional 20 minutes. Slice and serve.

Prep = 20 minutes **Cook** = 1 hour **Yield** = 12 servings

Strawberry Rhubarb Muffins

These are great muffins to cut in half, toast, and top with any of the jams in chapter 1. Inspired by strawberry-rhubarb pie, they are tart and tangy with the sweetness of peach liqueur for balance. Enjoy right out of the oven or make ahead, wrap, and store in a dry place for later.

- 2 ½ cups (275 g) all-purpose flour
- 2 teaspoons baking powder
- 1 teaspoon ground cinnamon
- ½ teaspoon ground nutmeg
- ¼ teaspoon ground cardamom
- 3 eggs
- ½ cup (100 g) granulated sugar
- 2 tablespoons (30 ml) peach liqueur
- ½ cup (120 ml) milk
- ¼ cup (60 g) sour cream
- 1 teaspoon pure vanilla extract
- 1 cup (170 g) chopped fresh or thawed frozen strawberries
- 1 cup (120 g) chopped fresh or thawed frozen rhubarb

Preheat the oven to 350°F (180°C, or gas mark 4). Spray a 6-cup muffin tin with nonstick cooking spray. In a bowl, whisk together the flour, baking powder, cinnamon, nutmeg, and cardamom. In a separate bowl, whisk the eggs with the sugar, peach liqueur, and milk until smooth and well combined. Add the sour cream and vanilla to the egg mixture and stir to combine. Add the wet ingredients to the dry, stirring with a wooden spoon to just combine. Add the strawberries and rhubarb and stir to combine. Spoon the muffin batter into the tin, filling each cup three-quarters of the way full. Bake until a toothpick inserted into the center of one muffin comes out clean, 30 to 40 minutes

Prep = 15 minutes **Cook** = 30 to 40 minutes **Yield** = 6 muffins

Soups, Salads, and Starters

Melon and Strawberry Salad with Midori Balsamic Vinaigrette

This salad of strawberries, melon, and grapes is best at the peak of all of the fruits' ripeness. Choose strawberries that are fragrant and deep red in color and melons that have a fresh and fruity scent. The riper the melons and strawberries, the sweeter the salad.

1 pound (455 g) fresh strawberries, hulled and halved
1 peeled and cubed yellow-fleshed melon, such as canary or Crenshaw
1 cup (150 g) red or green grapes, halved
  Zest of 1 lime
³/₄ cup (150 g) granulated sugar
2 tablespoons (8 g) chiffonaded mint leaves
2 teaspoons minced crystallized ginger
2 teaspoons white balsamic vinegar
1 tablespoon (15 ml) extra-virgin olive oil
2 teaspoons ginger liqueur, such as Domaine de Canton
1 tablespoon (15 ml) Midori
1 teaspoon minced fresh pineapple sage

In a large bowl, toss the strawberries, melon, and grapes with the lime zest, sugar, mint, and ginger. In a container with a lid, combine the vinegar, olive oil, ginger liqueur, Midori, and sage. Shake vigorously to combine. Pour over the fruit and toss to combine. Chill for at least 1 hour. Serve cold.

Prep = 20 minutes **Chill** = 1 hour **Yield** = 6 servings

Crab Bisque
with Pernod

Pernod is the French interpretation of a long-popular sipping liqueur, not overly sweet but with a nice balance of herbed anise flavors. Supported by fresh herbs, it lends a subtle touch to the inherent sweetness of crab bisque.

- 1 cup (130 g) frozen corn, thawed
- 1 tablespoon (14 g) unsalted butter
- 1 tablespoon (15 ml) canola oil
- 2 slices uncooked smoked bacon, chopped
- 3 large shallots, minced
- 2 bay leaves
- 4 cups (800 g) lump crabmeat, picked over for shells
- 1 teaspoon fennel seeds, crushed
- 1/2 cup (120 ml) Pernod
- 5 cups (1.2 L) fish or seafood stock
- 2 cups (475 ml) heavy cream
- 1 tablespoon (4 g) chopped fresh tarragon
- 1 tablespoon (4 g) chopped fresh flat-leaf parsley
- Salt and freshly ground pepper

Preheat oven to 400°F (200°C, or gas mark 6). Spray a sheet pan with olive oil or cooking spray. Place the corn on a sheet pan and roast for 20 minutes. Remove from the oven and set aside. In a large pot, melt the butter with the oil over medium-high heat. Add the bacon to the pot, cooking and stirring for 5 minutes, until it begins to brown. Add the shallots and bay leaves and sauté until the shallots are tender, about 3 minutes. Add the crab, roasted corn, and fennel seeds and cook, stirring, for 5 minutes. Add the Pernod and cook, stirring, for 5 minutes. Add the fish stock and heavy cream, bring to a boil, lower the heat to a simmer, and cook for 20 minutes. Stir in the tarragon and parsley, season with salt and black pepper, and cook for an additional 10 minutes. Discard the bay leaves. Serve warm.

Prep = 20 minutes **Cook** = 1 hour and 10 minutes
Yield = 8 servings

Watermelon Salad with Purple Basil, Feta, and Vanilla Liqueur

For a refreshing summertime treat, mix watermelon with feta cheese and add the tasty dressing in this recipe. Vanilla liqueur acts as the sweetener to the fresh basil and mint dressing. If you can't find purple basil, regular fresh green basil works just as well. But, fresh not dried makes all the difference.

- 1/3 cup (80 ml) extra-virgin olive oil
- 2 teaspoons freshly grated orange zest
- 2 tablespoons (30 ml) orange juice
- 2 teaspoons freshly ground sea salt
- 1/2 teaspoon freshly ground black pepper
- 1 (6- to 8-pound [2.7 to 3.6 k]) seedless watermelon, scooped into balls or cut into 1 1/2-inch (4 cm) cubes
- 1/2 cup (48 g) coarsely chopped mint leaves
- 1 tablespoon (4 g) chopped fresh purple basil
- 3 tablespoons (45 ml) vanilla liqueur
- 2 cups (300 g) crumbled feta cheese

Combine the oil, orange zest and juice, salt, and pepper in a container with a lid and shake vigorously to combine well. In a bowl, combine the watermelon with the mint, basil, and vanilla liqueur and toss. Place the watermelon mixture on a platter, drizzle with the dressing, and sprinkle with the feta cheese. Serve immediately.

Prep = 20 minutes **Yield** = 6 to 8 servings

Avocado Grapefruit Salad with Tequila Lime Vinaigrette

Grapefruit is a great fruit not often used as a salad component. The tartness of the citrus lends itself to a lightly sweetened and salty vinaigrette.

DRESSING:

- ½ cup (120 ml) extra-virgin olive oil
- 2 tablespoons (30 ml) fresh lime juice
- 1 tablespoon (15 ml) fresh orange juice
- ¼ cup (60 ml) white balsamic vinegar
- 2 tablespoons (30 ml) añejo tequila
- 1 teaspoon grated lime zest
- 2 teaspoons (10 g) honey
  Salt and freshly ground black pepper
- 2 tablespoons (8 g) finely chopped fresh cilantro
- 1 shallot, minced

SALAD:

- 2 ripe Haas avocados, peeled, seeds removed, thinly sliced
  Juice of 1 lime
- 1 red onion, very thinly sliced
- 4 cups (80 g) mixed salad greens
- 1 Ruby Red grapefruit, sectioned and membranes, pith, and seeds removed
- 6 sprigs fresh cilantro, for garnish
- ¼ cup (34 g) toasted pine nuts

For the dressing: Combine all the ingredients in a container with a tight-fitting lid and shake vigorously until emulsified.

For the salad: Place the sliced avocado in a small bowl and gently toss with the lime juice to prevent it from turning black. Place the salad greens in a large mixing bowl and toss with a generous amount of salad dressing. Place the greens on 6 salad plates and top with the avocado, grapefruit, and red onion. Garnish each with a cilantro sprig and pine nuts.

Prep = 15 minutes **Yield** = 6 servings

Shredded Chicken with Tomato Salsa Salad

This Limoncello-flavored recipe produces a simple and delicious salad that comes together quickly. If you have cooked chicken on hand, it will work fine; if not, simply poach or grill the chicken and shred.

2	cups (300 g) mixed yellow pear and red grape tomatoes, quartered
¼	cup (15 g) chopped fresh cilantro
2	tablespoons (8 g) shredded fresh basil
2	tablespoons (8 g) minced fresh chives
2	tablespoons (8 g) minced fresh mint
2	scallions, green and white parts, chopped
2	tablespoons (30 ml) Limoncello
1	tablespoon (15 ml) extra-virgin olive oil
	Freshly ground sea salt and black pepper
1	tablespoon (15 ml) white balsamic vinegar
2	(6-ounce [170 g]) chicken breasts, poached or grilled, shredded, and cooled
4	leaves Boston lettuce

In a large bowl, combine the tomatoes, cilantro, basil, chives, mint, scallions, Limoncello, oil, salt, pepper, and vinegar, and toss. Refrigerate for at least 30 minutes. Add the cooled chicken to the tomato mixture and toss to combine. Place 1 leaf of lettuce on each of 4 plates and top with the chicken salad. Serve cold.

Prep = 20 minutes **Cook** = 25 minutes (for poaching chicken)
Chill = 30 minutes **Yield** = 4 servings

Roasted Tomato and White Bean Soup

This tomato soup's pancetta, sage, smoked paprika, and spiced rum meld into a fantastic finale.

8   Roma tomatoes, halved
1   tablespoon (15 ml) olive oil, plus additional for tomatoes
     Freshly ground sea salt and black pepper
     Sour cream, for garnish
½   cup (75 g) diced pancetta
1   medium yellow onion, diced
3   cloves garlic, minced
3   cups (675 g) cooked and drained cannellini beans
8   fresh sage leaves, thinly sliced
1   teaspoon dried marjoram
1   teaspoon paprika
¼   cup (60 ml) sherry
½   cup (120 ml) spiced rum
3   tablespoons (45 g) tomato paste
4   cups (950 ml) chicken broth
1   tablespoon (4 g) chopped fresh basil, for garnish

Preheat the oven to 400°F (200°C, or gas mark 6). Place the tomato halves cut side up on an oiled sheet pan. Sprinkle each half with olive oil and season with salt and pepper. Place on the center rack of the oven and bake for 40 minutes, until beginning to brown on top and shrivel. In a stockpot, heat 1 tablespoon (15 ml) olive oil over medium-high heat. Add the pancetta and sauté until just turning golden brown. Add the onion and garlic and sauté until the onion is tender. Add the beans and sage and cook, stirring, for about 4 minutes. Lower the heat and add the tomatoes, marjoram, and paprika and cook, stirring, for 15 minutes. Add the sherry, spiced rum, and tomato paste and cook, stirring, for 15 minutes. Add the chicken broth, bring to a boil, lower the heat to a simmer, and cook for an additional 20 minutes. Using a stick blender, purée the mixture and season with salt and pepper. Strain through a fine-mesh sieve to produce a velvety bisque. Serve hot with a dollop of sour cream and a sprinkle of fresh basil.

Prep = 40 minutes **Cook** = 1 hour and 50 minutes
Yield = 6 servings

Sour Mash Black Bean Dip

This is a quick dish to enjoy right out of the pot. Sour mash whiskey is not sour at all but a well-rounded, consistent whiskey with a subtle yeastiness and smokiness under a rich caramel note. I like sour mash whiskey with the robust Mexican flavors of cumin and cayenne.

1	tablespoon (15 ml) vegetable oil
2	slices uncooked thick-cut bacon, chopped
1	medium yellow onion, chopped
3	cloves garlic, minced
2	(15-ounce [428 g]) cans black beans, 1 can drained
1	tablespoon (7 g) ground cumin
4	teaspoons (8 g) chili powder
1/8	teaspoon cayenne pepper
1/2	teaspoon freshly ground black pepper
1/2	cup (120 ml) sour mash whiskey
4	ounces (115 g) cream cheese
1/2	cup (55 g) grated sharp cheddar cheese
1	tablespoon (20 g) sour cream
2	tablespoons (8 g) chopped fresh cilantro
	Salt
	Tortilla chips for dipping

Heat the oil in a medium saucepan over medium-high heat. Add the bacon and cook until golden, about 4 minutes. Add the onion and sauté for 2 minutes, until tender and translucent. Add the garlic and cook for 2 minutes. Add the beans, cumin, chili powder, cayenne, and black pepper, stirring to combine, and cook for 3 minutes. Add the whiskey, stirring to incorporate, and cook for 3 minutes. Add the cream cheese and cheddar cheese, stirring to melt. Stir in the sour cream and cilantro. Season with salt and serve hot with tortilla chips. You can make the dip ahead of time, transfer to an ovenproof dish, cover, and refrigerate until ready to use. Once ready to serve, preheat the oven to 375°F (190°C, or gas mark 5), let the dip stand at room temperature for 10 minutes, then cover with foil and bake until hot and bubbling, about 20 minutes.

Prep = 10 minutes **Cook** = 20 minutes **Yield** = about 3 cups (780 g)

Caramelized Onion Soup with Calvados

The well-rounded flavors of apple brandy are dark and elegant with a touch of sweetened cider and vanilla bean, an excellent addition to slow-cooked foods.

- 1 tablespoon (15 ml) olive oil, plus extra for brushing
- 4 ounces (112 g) salt pork, cut into large cubes
- 4 pounds (1.8 k) sweet yellow onions, peeled and thinly sliced (about 6 onions)
- 2 tablespoons (25 g) granulated sugar
- 1 cup (235 ml) apple brandy, such as Laird's Applejack or Calvados
- ½ cup (120 ml) sherry
- 2 bay leaves
- 1 tablespoon (4 g) minced fresh thyme
- 8 cups (1,880 ml) good-quality beef broth
  Salt and freshly ground black pepper
  Olive oil, for brushing
- 1 loaf day-old brioche bread or French bread
- 2 cups (240 g) shredded Gruyère cheese

Heat the 1 tablespoon (15 ml) olive oil in a large soup pot over medium-high heat. Add the salt pork and render for 8 minutes. Remove the salt pork. Add the onions and stir to coat with the pan drippings. Lower the heat to low and cook the onions, stirring regularly, for 15 minutes. Add the sugar and continue to cook, stirring, for an additional 15 minutes, until the onions are cooked down and golden, not browned. Add the apple brandy and sherry, stirring to deglaze the pan. Cook for an additional 10 minutes. Add the thyme and beef broth, bring to a boil, lower the heat to low, and simmer for 20 minutes. Season with salt and black pepper. Preheat the broiler to high. Slice the bread into eight ½-inch (1.3 cm) -thick slices. Place on a sheet pan and brush with olive oil. Toast under the broiler until browned, only a couple of minutes. Sprinkle cheese evenly over top. Place soup bowls on a sheet pan and broil on middle oven rack until cheese is melted and browned. Serve the soup in individual soup bowls topped with croutons.

Prep = 15 minutes **Cook** = 1 hour and 15 minutes
Yield = 8 servings

White Bean and Garlic Soup with Grilled Sausage

Make this ahead of time, let cool completely, and refrigerate to allow the flavors to meld before reheating and serving.

5	links of your favorite pork sausage (about 1 pound [455 g])
3	tablespoons (45 ml) olive oil
4	slices uncooked bacon, chopped
1	Vidalia onion, chopped
2	stalks celery, chopped
1	yellow bell pepper, seeded and diced
4	cloves garlic, minced
2	(14½-ounce [412 g]) cans white cannellini beans
½	cup (120 ml) bourbon
4	cups (950 ml) chicken stock
¼	cup (60 ml) heavy cream
1	tablespoon (4 g) minced fresh flat-leaf parsley
1½	teaspoons fresh minced thyme
	Freshly ground sea salt and black pepper

Preheat the grill to high. Grill the sausages until cooked through, turning often. Transfer to a plate and set aside to cool. Once cool, slice into ¼-inch (6 mm) -thick pieces. In a large stockpot, heat the olive oil over medium-high heat. Add the bacon and cook for 5 minutes, just until the bacon browns. Add the sliced sausage, onion, celery, and yellow pepper and cook, stirring occasionally, until just tender. Add the garlic and both cans of beans, stir to combine, lower the heat to medium, and cook for 5 minutes. Add the bourbon and deglaze the pan. Add the chicken stock, parsley, and thyme, stirring to combine. Increase heat to a boil, then lower heat to medium and simmer for 30 minutes. Remove 2 cups (475 ml) of soup, place in a blender, and blend until smooth, being careful of the hot liquid rising and escaping from the lid. Add the puréed mixture back to the pot, add the cream, and stir. Season with salt and pepper. Serve hot.

Prep = 15 minutes **Cook** = 1 hour **Yield** = 6 servings

Vodka-Braised Artichoke and Olive Crostini

These crostini are a quick and easy party favorite. If you have a local Italian deli that stocks grilled or marinated artichoke hearts, they are certainly better than jarred—the better the quality, the more intense the flavor.

⅓ cup (80 ml) plus 2 tablespoons (30 ml) extra-virgin olive oil

2 (12-ounce [340 g]) jars marinated artichoke hearts, drained and chopped

¼ cup (28 g) pitted and chopped kalamata olives

2 tablespoons (6 g) minced sun-dried tomatoes

2 cloves garlic, minced

2 tablespoons (30 ml) lemon-flavored vodka

2 tablespoons (30 ml) white balsamic vinegar

Zest of 1 lemon

1 tablespoon (4 g) minced fresh flat-leaf parsley

1 teaspoon minced fresh mint

1 tablespoon (4 g) minced fresh basil

1 large French baguette, sliced on the diagonal into ¼-inch (6 mm) -thick slices

Preheat the oven to 350ºF (180ºC, or gas mark 4). In a large skillet, heat the 2 tablespoons (30 ml) of olive oil over medium heat. Add the artichokes, olives, and sun-dried tomatoes and sauté for 5 minutes, until the artichokes begin to turn golden. Add the garlic and cook for 2 minutes. Deglaze the pan with the lemon vodka, stirring to scrape up any bits on the bottom of the pan. Add the vinegar and lemon zest, stirring to combine. Remove from the heat and stir in the herbs. Set aside. Preheat broiler. Place the baguette slices on a sheet pan, brushing each piece generously with the remaining ⅓ cup (80 ml) olive oil. Place under the broiler, toasting until golden, about 3 minutes. Remove and serve the artichoke mixture on top of each crostini.

Prep = 30 minutes **Cook** = 15 minutes **Yield** = 4 appetizer servings

Chili con Queso with Whiskey

This traditional Mexican dish gets a darker, deeper boost from the addition of whiskey. If you can't find tomatoes canned with chiles, substitute canned tomatoes plus finely chopped fresh chiles to taste.

1 tablespoon (15 ml) olive oil

1 pound (455 g) ground chorizo

½ cup (80 g) chopped yellow onion

3 cloves garlic, minced

½ cup (120 ml) whiskey

1 (10-ounce [280 g]) can tomatoes with green chiles

1 (15- to 19-ounce [427 to 540 g]) can black beans, drained

1 (8-ounce [225 g]) block processed American cheese

½ cup (60 g) grated Monterey Jack cheese

Corn tortilla chips, for dipping

Heat the olive oil in a saucepan over medium heat. Add the chorizo and cook, stirring, for 5 minutes. Add the onion, stir, and sauté for 3 minutes. Add the garlic and cook for 2 minutes. Add the whiskey, stirring to combine. Add the tomatoes and black beans, stir, and continue to cook for 5 minutes. Add the cheeses, stirring until melted. Serve warm with corn tortilla chips.

Prep = 10 minutes **Cook** = 15 minutes **Yield** = about 4 cups (800 g)

Drunken Cocktail Wieners

This cocktail party dish is a winner: easy to make, easy to serve, and loaded with rich, vibrant flavor. The long cooking time is to meld the flavors and cook off the alcohol. Make the dish ahead of time to bring to any party, then just heat and serve.

    2   cups (480 g) ketchup
1 1/4   cups (295 ml) bourbon, such as Jim Beam brand
    1   cup (100 g) confectioners' sugar
  1/2   cup (112 g) packed light brown sugar
    1   tablespoon (15 ml) Worcestershire sauce
  1/2   cup (80 g) chopped sweet yellow onion
    2   pounds (910 g) cocktail franks or hot dogs cut into 1 1/2-inch
        (4 cm) pieces

Combine all ingredients in a large saucepan over medium heat and bring to a slow boil, stirring occasionally. Lower the heat and simmer for 1 hour, stirring occasionally. Serve hot or cold as an appetizer. Bring these as a treat to any party by placing the cooked product into a slow cooker. Just plug in and warm once you've arrived.

Prep = 10 minutes **Cook** = 1 hour **Yield** = 20 appetizer servings

Bell Pepper Crostini

I enjoy serving small plates of a variety of dishes when I'm entertaining. I like my guests to have a selection of several dishes rather than a few. Small plates, or *tapas* as they are called today, are a great way to do this. These bell pepper crostini are a great addition to any small plate menu. They are easy to prepare and packed with flavor.

- 6 cloves garlic, roasted (see note)
- 2 tablespoons (30 ml) extra-virgin olive oil, plus additional for roasting the garlic, and brushing the peppers and bread
- 1 red bell pepper
- 1 yellow bell pepper
- 1 orange bell pepper
- 1 bulb fennel, very thinly sliced
- 1 tablespoon (8.6 g) capers, drained
- 2 tablespoons (30 ml) plus 1 teaspoon (5 ml) anisette liqueur
- 1 tablespoon plus 1 teaspoon (5 g) fresh flat-leaf parsley, minced
- 1 teaspoon minced fresh lemon thyme
  Freshly ground sea salt and black pepper
- 1 fresh baguette or ciabatta, sliced into thin crostini, brushed with olive oil and toasted on one side
- 6 ounces (168 g) good-quality goat cheese, softened
- ¼ cup (25 g) grated Parmigiano-Reggiano cheese

Roast the garlic, as instructed below. Brush the bell peppers lightly with olive oil. Roast on a grill, under the broiler or over the flame of a gas stove, charring the skin. Once the skin is charred, place the peppers in a paper bag and close, letting them rest for 5 minutes (this will aid in removing the skin). Remove the peppers from the bag, clean away the charred skin, slice open, and remove their seeds and membranes. Slice the peppers thinly and set aside. In a skillet, heat the 2 tablespoons (30 ml) olive oil over medium-high heat. Add the fennel and sauté until tender, about 3 minutes. Add the roasted peppers, roasted garlic, and capers and sauté for 2 minutes, mashing the roasted garlic into the oil and stirring to combine the flavors. Deglaze the pan with the 2 tablespoons (30 ml) anisette and cook for an additional 2 minutes to cook off the alcohol. Remove from the heat and stir in the parsley and thyme. Season with salt and black pepper and set aside. Preheat broiler. Place the baguette slices on a sheet pan, brushing each piece generously with olive oil. Place under the broiler, toasting until golden, about 3 minutes. Remove and increase the broiler heat to high. In a small bowl mash the goat cheese with the Parmigiano and the remaining teaspoon of anisette. Spread the goat cheese mixture on each crostini and place on a sheet pan. Return the crostini to the broiler just to brown the goat cheese a bit. Arrange the crostini on a serving platter, topping each with the pepper mixture. Serve warm.

To roast the garlic: Preheat oven to 375°F (190°C, or gas mark 5). Cut away the top of a whole head of garlic, enough just to reveal the garlic inside. Place the cloves in a shallow, ovenproof pan with a cover or in a garlic-roasting dish. Drizzle with extra-virgin olive oil, place in oven, and roast for about 30 minutes, until the cloves are browned, soft, and fragrant. Remove from the oven; set aside to cool completely. The cloves will pull away from the skin and come out if you push from the bottom with your fingers, or use a small cocktail fork or spoon. Store the garlic in an airtight container in the refrigerator up to 10 days. Alternatively, remove the individual cloves from the skins, pack cloves in olive oil in an airtight container, and store in the refrigerator up to one month.

Prep = 30 minutes **Cook** = 45 minutes **Yield** = 4 to 6 servings

Scallop Ceviche
with Tequila Cream

Popular in most of Latin America, ceviche is always a combination of finfish or shellfish with a citrus marinade; the citrus denatures or "cooks" the proteins in the seafood.

- ⅓ cup (80 ml) fresh orange juice
- ¼ cup (60 ml) fresh lemon juice
- 3 tablespoons (45 ml) fresh lime juice
- Pinch of kosher salt
- ½ teaspoon granulated sugar
- 1 pound (455 g) large scallops, chopped
- 12 cherry tomatoes, stems removed, quartered
- 2 tablespoons (28 g) seeded and finely chopped red bell pepper
- 2 tablespoons (28 g) seeded and finely chopped yellow bell pepper
- 1 small, ripe Haas avocado, peeled, seeded, and cubed
- ½ small red onion, slivered
- ½ cup (50 g) cubed English cucumber
- 1 serrano chile, minced
- 2 tablespoons (8 g) chopped fresh cilantro
- 2 tablespoons (41 g) sour cream
- 2 tablespoons (30 ml) gold tequila
- Salt and freshly ground black pepper
- 4 sprigs fresh cilantro
- Corn chips, for serving

In a nonreactive bowl, stir together the orange, lemon, and lime juices. Season with salt and sugar to balance the acid of the citrus juices. Add the scallops to the citrus mixture, stirring to combine. Cover and refrigerate for 1 hour. In a bowl, combine the tomatoes, red and yellow pepper, avocado, onion, cucumber, chile, and chopped cilantro and stir gently to combine. Transfer the scallops to a colander and let drain for several seconds, then add the fish to the tomato mixture and mix gently. In a small bowl, stir together the sour cream and tequila, then add to the scallop mixture, stirring gently to combine. Season with salt and pepper. Divide the ceviche among martini glasses or small glass bowls and garnish with the cilantro sprigs. Serve immediately with corn chips.

Prep = 20 minutes **Chill** = 1 hour **Yield** = 4 servings

Lobster Guacamole with Coconut Rum

If you can cook the lobster at home, use some of its juices in the guacamole. If time isn't on your side, you can use lobster meat from your local seafood shop.

4   pounds (1.8 k) live lobsters or 1 pound (455 g) lobster meat
4   ripe avocados
1   tomato, seeded and shopped
½   cup (80 g) chopped Vidalia onion
1   jalapeño pepper, seeded and minced
3   tablespoons (12 g) chopped fresh cilantro
    Juice of 1 lime
1   yellow bell pepper, seeded and chopped
1   tablespoon (15 ml) coconut-flavored rum
1   tablespoon (4 g) chopped fresh chives
    Freshly ground sea salt and black pepper
    Tortilla chips or wonton chips for dipping

Fill the bottom of a large stockpot with a tight-fitting lid with about ¾ inch (2 cm) of water. Bring the water to boil over high heat. Once steaming, add the lobsters to the pot and cover tightly. Steam for 20 minutes. Remove from the pot and plunge into a large bowl full of ice water, until cooled. Remove the lobsters from the water and drain. Clean the meat from the lobsters, reserving the juices. Chop the meat and set aside. Strain the lobster juice through a fine-mesh sieve to get ¼ cup (60 ml) of lobster juice and set aside. Cut the avocados in half lengthwise and remove the seeds. Remove the flesh from the skin and chop, placing in a large bowl. Add the tomato, onion, jalapeño, cilantro, and one-third of the lobster meat. Using a potato masher, mash the mixture to combine and gently smash the avocado. Add the lime juice, reserved ¼ cup (60 ml) lobster juice, yellow pepper, coconut rum, chives, and remaining lobster meat. Season with salt and black pepper and stir to combine. Cover with plastic wrap and chill for at least 30 minutes and up to overnight. If chilling overnight, drop two of the avocado seeds into the guacamole to keep it from turning black. Serve the guacamole with tortilla chips or as an appetizer on fried wonton chips.

Prep = 30 minutes **Cook** = 20 minutes (if using live lobsters only)
Chill = at least 30 minutes **Yield** = about 6 cups (1.2 kg)

Blueberry-Avocado Salad with Limoncello

Avocados are a great source of good fats and nutrients. I can eat them just sprinkled with salt and pepper as a snack any time. Here, as a salad, the avocado takes center stage with a combination of sweet, tart, and citrus. Mangoes, blueberries, and a splash of Limoncello come together as a fresh, delightful snack or salad.

2   ripe avocados, peeled and diced
1   ripe mango peeled, cored, and diced
½   pint (150 g) fresh blueberries
1   yellow bell pepper washed and sliced into thin strips
1   tablespoon (15 ml) fresh orange juice
1   tablespoon (15 ml) fresh lemon juice
1   tablespoon (15 ml) extra-virgin olive oil
1   tablespoon (15 ml) Limoncello
    Freshly ground sea salt and black pepper
    Corn chips or mixed greens for serving

In a bowl, toss together all ingredients, seasoning with salt and pepper. Place in an airtight container and refrigerate for 30 minutes. Serve as an appetizer with corn chips or as a salad on a bed of mixed greens.

Prep = 15 minutes   **Chill** = 30 minutes   **Yield** = 4 to 6 servings

SoCo Crab Party Dip

Tender, sweet crab pairs great with the unique flavors of Southern Comfort. First developed in New Orleans, Louisiana, in the mid-1800s, Southern Comfort combines notes of lemon, vanilla bean, cinnamon, and orange with other herbs and spices. If it isn't available, an orange liqueur will be a fine substitute.

- 2 tablespoons (30 ml) olive oil
- 1 shallot, minced
- 2 cloves garlic, minced
- 8 ounces (225 g) lump crabmeat picked over for shells
- 1 tablespoon (4 g) chopped fresh flat-leaf parsley
- 4 ounces (58 g) cream cheese, softened
- 1/4 cup (60 ml) Southern Comfort
- 1/2 teaspoon hot sauce
- 1 cup (115 g) shredded Monterey Jack cheese
- 1/2 teaspoon ancho chile powder
- 1/2 teaspoon Old Bay seasoning
- Salt and freshly ground black pepper
- Tortilla chips, for serving

Heat the olive oil in a medium saucepan over medium-high heat. Add the shallot and garlic and sauté until tender and the shallot turns translucent, about 3 minutes. Add the crabmeat and sauté for 4 minutes, stirring constantly. Add the Southern Comfort and deglaze the pan, then cook down, stirring, for 4 minutes. Add the cream cheese, Monterey Jack, ancho chile powder, hot sauce, and Old Bay, stirring to melt the cheeses. Stir in the parsley, season to taste with salt and black pepper, and serve warm with tortilla chips. The dip can be made ahead of time, transferred to an ovenproof dish, covered, and refrigerated until ready to serve. Once ready to serve, let stand for 10 minutes at room temperature. Preheat the oven to 375°F (190°C, or gas mark 5). Cover the dip with aluminum foil and bake for 20 minutes, until bubbling and hot.

Prep = 10 minutes **Cook** = 16 minutes
Yield = about 3 cups (710 g)

SoCo and Tea Brined Chicken Wings

Yes, you are reading this right. This dish brines chicken in equal amounts of Southern Comfort and tea, for a tasty and comforting starter or snack.

2   cups (475 ml) Southern Comfort

2   cups (475 ml) brewed tea

1   orange, thinly sliced

½   cup (150 g) kosher or sea salt

1   tablespoon (5 g) black peppercorns

½   cup (112 g) firmly packed brown sugar

1   bay leaf

1   sprig fresh rosemary

3   pounds (1.4 k) chicken wings, sectioned

2   tablespoons (30 ml) olive oil

    Freshly ground black pepper

2   tablespoons (40 g) honey

In a large pot over high heat, combine the Southern Comfort, tea, orange slices, salt, peppercorns, sugar, bay leaf, and rosemary. Simmer until the salt and sugar are dissolved. Remove from the heat and let cool for 20 minutes. Chill until completely cooled, then add the chicken wings, cover, and refrigerate for at least 12 hours and up to 24 hours. Preheat grill to high heat. Remove the wings from the brine, rinse, and pat dry. Place the wings in a large bowl and toss with the olive oil, coating evenly. Season with black pepper. Grill the wings until cooked through, turning occasionally, about 20 minutes. Transfer to a bowl, drizzle with honey, and toss to coat evenly. Serve hot.

Prep = 30 minutes + 12 hours to soak in brine   **Cook** = 20 minutes
Yield = 4 to 6 servings

Italian Wedding Soup

The name "Wedding Soup" actually derived from a mistranslation of an Italian dish, *minestra maritata* means "married soup," and refers to the marriage of meats and vegetables in broth. Today's wedding soup is much lighter than the original, which is believed to derive from a Spanish combination of various meats and greens. Deglazing the pan with brandy adds smoothness and a depth of flavor.

2	tablespoons (30 ml) extra-virgin olive oil
4	carrots, cut into 1/2-inch (1.2 cm) dice
2	stalks celery, chopped
1	small yellow onion, minced
3	cloves garlic, minced
2 1/2	quarts (2.4 L) chicken broth
2	cups (475 ml) water
1	bunch kale, stems removed, leaves cut into thin strips
1	pound (455 g) ground pork
1	medium sweet onion, chopped
2	tablespoons (8 g) minced fresh flat-leaf parsley
1/4	cup (25 g) grated Pecorino Romano cheese
1/4	cup (25 g) grated Parmigiano-Reggiano cheese, plus more for serving
2	eggs, lightly beaten
1/2	cup (60 g) fresh bread crumbs
1/2	teaspoon salt, plus more to taste
1/2	teaspoon freshly ground black pepper, plus more to taste
2	tablespoons (30 ml) vegetable oil
1/4	cup (60 ml) brandy (plus more, if necessary, for multiple batches)
1	(14 1/2-ounce [412 g]) can white beans, drained

Heat the olive oil in a 5-quart (4.7 L) Dutch oven over medium-high heat. Add the carrots, celery, and yellow onion and sauté until the carrots are tender, about 7 minutes. Add the garlic and cook for 2 minutes. Add the brandy and cook for 2 minutes, stirring to scrape up any bits from the bottom of the pan. Add the broth, water, and kale, bring to a boil for 2 minutes, then reduce the heat to a simmer and cook for 30 minutes. Meanwhile, in a large bowl, combine the ground pork, sweet onion, Pecorino Romano, 1/4 cup (25 g) Parmigiano cheese, parsley, eggs, bread crumbs, 1/2 teaspoon salt, and 1/2 teaspoon pepper. Mix with your hands, form into 1-inch (2.5 cm) balls, and place on a plate. In a large skillet over medium-high heat, warm the vegetable oil. Add the meatballs, being careful not to over-crowd the pan (work in batches if necessary, using additional brandy) and cook until browned, about 5 minutes per side. Toss the meatballs around in the pan to absorb the flavor of the brandy. Transfer the meatballs to a paper towel-lined plate to drain. Add the meatballs and the white beans to the soup and simmer until the meatballs are cooked through, about 15 minutes. Adjust the seasonings with salt and pepper. Ladle the soup into warmed bowls and serve immediately. Pass the extra grated Parmigiano cheese at the table.

Prep = 20 minutes **Cook** = 1 hour and 15 minutes
Yield = 8 servings

4

Poultry

Coq au Vin

I know the use of spirits in this classic is small compared to that of wine, but it would be unjust not to include this iconic dish. Cognac is the traditional choice, but Armagnac and other brandies are interchangeable. Use what is in your liquor cabinet or the one you prefer.

1 large roasting chicken, cut into 8 serving pieces
  Freshly ground sea salt and black pepper
4 tablespoons (½ stick, or 55 g) unsalted butter
4 slices uncooked smoked bacon, chopped
2 medium sweet yellow onions, diced
1 large carrot, peeled and diced
3 cloves garlic, minced
4 shallots, peeled and chopped
10 ounces (280 g) button mushrooms, cleaned, stems trimmed
3 tablespoons (21 g) all-purpose flour
1 (750 ml) bottle red wine
3 tablespoons (45 ml) cognac
4 cups (950 ml) chicken stock

Season the chicken pieces generously with salt and black pepper. In a large casserole pot with a lid, heat the butter and bacon over medium-high heat. Cook until the bacon begins to turn brown, about 7 minutes. Transfer the bacon to a plate. Add the chicken pieces, skin side down, and brown on both sides, about 4 minutes per side. Transfer the chicken to the plate with the bacon. To the casserole add the onions and carrot and sauté until just tender, about 5 minutes. Add the garlic, shallots, and mushrooms and cook for 2 minutes. Add the chicken and bacon back to the pan, sprinkle all with the flour, turning to coat, and cook for 2 minutes. Pour in the wine and cognac, stirring to combine and thicken. Add the chicken stock, bring to a boil, lower the heat, and simmer for 1 hour, until the chicken is cooked through and tender. Transfer the chicken to a serving bowl. Bring the sauce to a boil, lower the heat, and simmer for 10 minutes to just thicken, then season with salt and black pepper to taste. Pour over the chicken and serve.

Prep = 20 minutes **Cook** = 1 hour and 35 minutes
Yield = 8 servings

Cuban Chicken with Pineapple

Island dishes are packed with flavor because of the freshness and variety of fruits and vegetables available in the tropics.

1	(4-pound [1.8 kg]) roasting chicken, cut into 8 serving pieces
	Grated zest and juice of 2 limes
	Salt and freshly ground black pepper
1/4	cup (60 ml) olive oil
1	medium yellow onion, chopped
2	cloves garlic, chopped
1	(14 1/2-ounce [412 g]) can diced tomatoes
1/4	cup (41 g) golden raisins
1	red hot pepper, seeded and minced
1/4	teaspoon dried oregano
1	stick cinnamon
1	bay leaf
1	cup (235 ml) chicken stock
2	cups (300 g) coarsely chopped fresh pineapple and its juice
1/4	cup (60 ml) golden rum

Preheat oven to 375°F (190°C, or gas mark 5). Place the chicken pieces in a mixing bowl. Rub the lime zest, juice, salt, and pepper over the chicken pieces, then set aside for 30 minutes. In a large Dutch oven, heat the olive oil over medium-high heat. Brown the chicken pieces on all sides. Transfer the chicken to a dish as it is browned. Once all chicken is removed, add the onion and garlic and sauté until tender, about 3 minutes. Add the tomatoes, raisins, hot pepper, oregano, cinnamon stick, and bay leaf, and cook for 5 minutes. Stir in the chicken stock and add the chicken back to the pan, spooning the sauce all over the chicken. Cover and bake for 30 minutes. Remove the cover and bake for an additional 15 minutes. Meanwhile, place the pineapple and any juices in a small saucepan over medium heat, and reduce the liquid by half. Add the rum and cook for 2 minutes. Pour over the chicken and bake for an additional 5 minutes, or until an instant-read thermometer inserted into the thickest part of one of the breasts reads at least 165°F (74°C). Remove from the oven, discard cinnamon stick and bay leaf, and serve.

Prep = 40 minutes including marinating **Cook** = 1 hour
Yield = 4 to 6 servings

Coconut Rum and Pineapple Chicken

Once again, coconut, rum, and pineapple come together, here as a cooked salsa that develops an incredible combination of flavors in one skillet. Be sure to deglaze the pan as you add the rum, as so much flavor is found stuck to the bottom of the skillet during cooking.

2   (8-ounce [225 g]) boneless, skinless chicken breasts, split in half horizontally
    Salt and freshly ground black pepper

MARINADE:
¼   cup (60 ml) coconut milk
¼   cup (60 ml) pineapple juice (from canned pineapple below)
2   tablespoons (30 ml) fresh lime juice
3   tablespoons (45 ml) Madras curry sauce
3   tablespoons (45 ml) extra-virgin olive oil

SAUCE:
1   red onion, halved and thinly sliced
4   cloves garlic, chopped
½   cup (120 ml) coconut-flavored rum
1   tablespoon (15 ml) pineapple juice
½   cup (120 ml) coconut milk
2   tablespoons (30 ml) fresh lime juice
1   (15-ounce [428 g]) can cubed or chopped pineapple in juice
1   tablespoon (4 g) coarsely chopped fresh basil
1   tablespoon (4 g) minced fresh cilantro

Season each chicken breast on both sides with salt and black pepper. Place the chicken in a sealable container.

For the marinade: In a small bowl, combine the coconut milk, pineapple juice, lime juice, and Madras sauce. Pour the marinade over the chicken, cover, and refrigerate for 1 hour. Remove from the refrigerator 10 minutes prior to cooking. Heat the oil in a large skillet over medium-high heat and add the chicken breasts, draining some of the excess marinade off of each piece. Cook until browned, about 7 minutes per side. Transfer the chicken to a plate.

For the sauce: Add the onion to the skillet and sauté until translucent, about 7 minutes. Add the garlic and cook for 3 minutes. Deglaze the pan with the coconut rum, cooking for 2 minutes. Add the pineapple juice, coconut milk, lime juice, and pineapple with its juice. Cook for 5 minutes, to let the sauce reduce. Add the chicken back to the pan with any juices that have accumulated on the plate. Add the basil and cilantro, stir to combine, and serve with rice.

Prep = 1 hour, including marinating time   **Cook** = 30 minutes
Yield = 4 servings

Mexican Chicken and Black Bean Casserole

This colorful casserole uses tequila and Mexican cheese to spark its authentic flavors.

2 cloves garlic, minced
¼ cup (60 ml) extra-virgin olive oil
¼ cup (60 ml) red wine vinegar
2 tablespoons (30 ml) añejo or reposado tequila
1 teaspoon freshly grated lime zest
 Juice of ½ lime
1 tablespoon (7 g) ground cumin
⅛ teaspoon ground cinnamon
2 teaspoons chili powder
1 tablespoon (4 g) dried oregano
2 (8-ounce [225 g]) boneless, skinless chicken breasts
1 cup (112 g) roughly crumbled tricolored corn tortilla chips
1 (14½-ounce [412 g]) can black beans, drained
6 ounces (142 g) crumbled Mexican cheese
4 ounces (115 g) grated sharp cheddar cheese

In a resealable plastic bag or container, combine the garlic, olive oil, red wine vinegar, tequila, lime zest and juice, cumin, cinnamon, chili powder, and oregano. Add the chicken, seal, and shake vigorously to coat evenly. Set aside to marinade for 30 minutes; if marinating longer than 30 minutes, refrigerate. Remove the chicken from the refrigerator and let stand for 10 minutes before cooking. Preheat the grill to high heat. Spray a 9 × 13-inch (23 × 33 cm) baking pan with nonstick cooking spray. Grill or sauté the chicken breasts until cooked through, about 7 minutes per side. Transfer to a plate to cool. Preheat oven to 350°F (180°C, or gas mark 4). When cool, shred the chicken into small strips. Spread ½ cup (56 g) of the tortilla chips on the bottom of the baking pan, top with half the shredded chicken, half the black beans, and half of each of the cheeses, spreading each ingredient evenly in layers. Repeat with the remaining chips, chicken, and beans, finishing with the cheeses. Place in the oven and bake until bubbling and the cheese is melted, about 30 minutes. Serve hot with a side of Spanish rice.

Prep = 40 minutes **Cook** = 45 minutes **Yield** = 6 servings

Bourbon Hot Wings

My version of the Buffalo classic, these hot wings are quick and simple. You decide which and how much hot sauce to use. You'll be surprised at the subtle but elegant flavor that the sour mash whiskey develops in the pan with the butter and hot sauce.

- 2 quarts (1.9 L) vegetable or canola oil, for frying
- 4 pounds (1.8 k) chicken wings, divided into two sections, wing tips discarded
- 2 tablespoons (28 g) unsalted butter
- 1 cup (235 ml) hot sauce (I prefer Frank's brand)
- 1 tablespoon (15 ml) sour mash whiskey, such as Jack Daniels

Heat the oil in a large, deep stockpot to 375°F (190°C). Wash the wings and pat dry. Place the wings in the oil gently, being careful of the rising steam and bubbles. Do not overload the pot; it may be necessary to fry the wings in a few batches. Fry the wings for 8 minutes to cook through, 10 if you like them crispy, then drain and transfer to a mixing bowl. In a saucepan, melt the butter with the hot sauce, add the whiskey, and stir to combine. Pour the hot sauce over the wings, tossing to coat evenly. Serve with cold blue cheese dressing and celery and carrot sticks.

Prep = 15 minutes **Cook** = 8 to 10 minutes per batch
Yield = 6 servings

Galliano Chicken

Galliano is a unique blend of bark, herbs, plants, roots, and flowers which add subtle flavors.

4   (8-ounce [225 g]) boneless, skinless chicken breasts
    Freshly ground sea salt and black pepper
4   cloves garlic, minced
¼   cup (60 ml) extra-virgin olive oil
2   tablespoons (28 g) unsalted butter
1   red onion, halved and thinly sliced
1   cup (150 g) halved red grapes
2   shallots, minced
½   cup (120 ml) Galliano liqueur
¼   cup (60 ml) fresh orange juice
½   cup (120 ml) chicken stock
1   tablespoon (4 g) minced fresh flat-leaf parsley
1   tablespoon (4 g) chopped fresh basil

Butterfly the chicken breasts by laying them flat on a clean, dry cutting board. Working with a sharp boning or chef's knife, with the thickest end of the chicken facing you, slice the breasts in half horizontally being careful not to cut all the way through. Open up the breasts to resemble two butterfly wings. If necessary, cover with plastic wrap and pound lightly to make the breasts a consistent thickness. Season generously on both sides with salt and black pepper. Place the chicken in a sealable container or resealable plastic bag. Add the garlic and 2 tablespoons (30 ml) of the olive oil, seal, and toss the chicken around in the oil and garlic, then set aside for 30 minutes. In a large skillet, melt the butter with the remaining 2 tablespoons (30 ml) of olive oil over medium-high heat. Add the chicken pieces and brown for 5 minutes per side. Transfer the chicken to a plate. Add the red onion to the skillet and sauté for 5 minutes, until turning tender and translucent. Add the grapes and shallots, stir, and sauté for 5 minutes. Deglaze the pan with the Galliano and orange juice, scraping up any bits on the bottom of the skillet. Add the chicken back to the pan, add the chicken stock, and bring to a boil. Turn the chicken a couple of times in the sauce, cooking for an additional 5 minutes. Transfer the chicken to individual plates. Add the parsley and basil to the sauce and cook, stirring, for an additional 4 minutes. Spoon the sauce over the chicken and serve.

Prep = 40 minutes including marinating **Cook** = 30 minutes
Yield = 4 servings

Añejo-Roasted Chicken

The dry rub can be used for other baked and grilled meats as well.

1	(3- to 4-pound [2.1 to 1.8 kg]) whole chicken or in-bone breasts
2	teaspoons ground cumin
1	teaspoon dried oregano
1	teaspoon Spanish paprika
1/2	teaspoon ancho chile powder
1	teaspoon salt
1	teaspoon freshly ground black pepper
7	tablespoons (105 ml) olive oil
1	Vidalia onion, chopped
1	green bell pepper, seeded and chopped
8	cloves garlic, smashed
2	bay leaves
3/4	cup (175 ml) añejo tequila
1	(14 1/2-ounce [412 g]) can fire-roasted, diced tomatoes
1/2	cup (110 g) salsa verde (green salsa)
	Juice of 2 limes
1	cup (235 ml) chicken stock
7	sprigs fresh cilantro

Preheat the oven to 375°F (190°C, or gas mark 5). Wash and remove the insides from the chicken. Pat dry and cut into 6 serving pieces, leaving the leg and thigh sections together. Place in a large mixing bowl. Combine the cumin, oregano, paprika, ancho chile powder, salt, and pepper. Rub into the chicken thoroughly, getting under the skin. Let sit for 15 minutes. Heat 1/4 cup (60 ml) of the olive oil in a lidded braising pan large enough to accommodate the chicken. Brown the chicken on all sides. Transfer to a bowl. Add the remaining 3 tablespoons (45 ml) of olive oil to the pan. Add the onion and pepper and sauté for 3 minutes. Add the garlic and bay leaves and cook for an additional 2 minutes. Deglaze the pan with the tequila, stirring to scrape up any bits from the bottom of the pan. Bring to a boil and cook for 2 minutes. Add the tequila, tomatoes, salsa verde, lime juice, and chicken stock and cook for 5 minutes. Add the cilantro, stirring to incorporate. Add the chicken pieces back to the pan and bring the liquid to a boil. Cover and place in the oven. Cook for 1 hour, or until the meat can be pulled away from the bones. Remove from the oven and serve over beans and rice.

Prep = 30 minutes including marinating
Cook = 1 hour and 20 minutes   **Yield** = 4 servings

Tequila-Braised Bone-In Chicken Breast

From Grady Spear's *A Cowboy in the Kitchen*, this braised chicken recipe was originally for pheasant.

4	bone-in chicken breasts (about 2 pounds [910 g])
	Freshly ground sea salt and black pepper
	Zest of 2 oranges (pith removed)
1/3	cup (80 ml) virgin olive oil
1	sweet yellow onion, chopped
4	cloves garlic, chopped
1	tablespoon (7 g) all-purpose flour
1	cup (235 ml) añejo tequila
1/4	cup (60 ml) chicken stock
1	teaspoon chopped fresh rosemary
1	tablespoon (4 g) chopped fresh thyme
2	bay leaves
4	peaches, peeled, pitted, and halved
1/2	cup (120 ml) dry red wine
2	whole cloves
2	tablespoons (25 g) granulated sugar

Preheat the oven to 400°F (200°C, or gas mark 6). Rub the chicken breasts thoroughly with salt and pepper, getting under the skin. Work the orange zest under the skin of each breast. Heat the oil over medium heat in an ovenproof casserole. Brown the chicken on all sides, transfer to a plate. Add the onion and garlic and sauté for 2 minutes, until tender. Sprinkle the flour over all and cook for 1 minute, until it begins to brown. Add the tequila and stock, stirring as the sauce thickens. Add the chicken breasts to the casserole, coating with the sauce. Sprinkle the breasts with the rosemary and thyme. Add the bay leaves and the peach halves. Cover and place on the middle rack of the oven and bake for 45 minutes, until an instant-read thermometer pierced into the center of one of the breasts reads 165°F (74°C). Remove from the oven and transfer the chicken to a serving platter; cover to keep hot. Strain the braising liquid into a saucepan over medium heat, pressing the peaches to extract the juices. Add the red wine, cloves, and sugar. Bring to a boil, then reduce the heat to a simmer. Reduce the sauce for 5 minutes to thicken. Serve with sauce.

Prep = 20 minutes   **Cook** = 1 hour   **Yield** = 4 servings

Chicken on a Bottle

As odd as this may seem, this technique is a perfect use of an empty (or half full) liquor bottle. The trick is indirect cooking that allows the chicken to slowly seal in its own juices while letting go of its fat, with the spiced rum in the bottle pouring flavor from the inside out.

1   (4- to 4 ½-pound [1.8 to 2 kg]) chicken, washed inside and out and patted dry
1   tablespoon (15 ml) extra-virgin olive oil
1   teaspoon freshly ground sea salt
2   teaspoons freshly ground black pepper
1   cup (235 ml) spiced rum or bourbon
2   cups Smoked Bourbon BBQ Sauce (page 33)

Preheat grill for indirect cooking to high heat. Brush the chicken with olive oil and season with salt and pepper. Select an oven-safe liquor bottle short enough to hold the chicken upright inside the grill. Pour the spiced rum into the bottle. Place on the grill on a high-sided sheet pan, positioning the bottle in the center of the pan. Place the chicken on the bottle with the wings facing upward. Brush the chicken thoroughly with the barbecue sauce. Roast for 30 minutes, turn the chicken, baste again, and continue to cook for an additional 30 minutes, or until the internal temperature (check with an instant-read thermometer) has reached 170°F (77°C). Transfer the chicken to a cutting board and let rest for 10 minutes. Carve into serving pieces, brushing each with any remaining barbecue sauce, and serve.

Prep = 10 minutes   **Cook** = 1 hour   **Yield** = 6 to 8 servings

Thyme Chicken with Bourbon

The contrasting flavors meld into a complex sauce.

4	(8-ounce [225 g]) boneless, skinless chicken breasts
7	tablespoons (105 ml) extra-virgin olive oil
3 ½	tablespoons (70 g) honey
3	tablespoons (45 ml) balsamic vinegar
1	tablespoon (4 g) fresh minced thyme
	Salt and black pepper
¼	cup (38 g) diced pancetta
1	poblano pepper, seeded and thinly sliced
2	large peaches, peeled, pitted, and thinly sliced
1	tablespoon (14 g) light brown sugar
¼	cup (60 ml) bourbon
1	tablespoon (14 g) unsalted butter
1	tablespoon (4 g) minced fresh flat-leaf parsley

Working with a sharp boning knife, butterfly the chicken breasts, slicing in half horizontally—do not cut all the way through. Open up the breasts to resemble two butterfly wings. If necessary, cover with plastic wrap and pound lightly so the breasts are a consistent thickness. In a sealable container, combine 4 tablespoons (60 ml) of the olive oil with 2 tablespoons of the honey, the balsamic vinegar, and 2 teaspoons (40 g) of thyme. Seal and shake vigorously. Season both sides of each chicken breast with salt and pepper. Place the chicken breasts back in the container, turning to coat with marinade. Set aside for 30 minutes. Heat the remaining 3 tablespoons (45 ml) olive oil in a large skillet over medium-high heat. Remove the chicken from the marinade, drain, place in the skillet, and brown on both sides, about 5 minutes per side. Transfer to a plate. Add the diced pancetta to the skillet and cook until browned, about 7 minutes. Add the poblano pepper and peaches and cook for 3 minutes. Add the brown sugar and bourbon, scraping the bottom of the pan to deglaze. Cook for 3 minutes. Add the remaining honey, thyme, butter, and parsley, stirring until the butter has melted. Add the chicken and any juices back to the pan, and cook for an additional 5 minutes, turning once. Serve the chicken topped with sauce.

Prep = 40 minutes including marinating **Cook** = 30 minutes
Yield = 4 servings

Shredded Chicken Añejo

This crowd-pleasing casserole with chicken, vegetables, and tortilla chips will feed the masses.

- 3 pounds (1.4 kg) boneless, skinless chicken breasts, washed and patted dry, sliced in half horizontally
- Salt and freshly ground black pepper
- 3 cloves garlic, minced
- 1 tablespoon (4 g) dried oregano
- 1/4 cup (60 ml) plus 2 tablespoons (28 ml) añejo tequila
- 4 tablespoons (60 ml) extra-virgin olive oil
- 1 1/2 teaspoons ground cumin
- 1 1/2 teaspoons chili powder
- 1 (28-ounce [800 g]) can diced tomatoes, drained
- 1 (14 1/2-ounce [412 g]) can hominy, drained
- 1 cup (130 g) frozen or drained canned corn
- 1/4 cup (40 g) sliced pickled jalapeños
- 6 cups (168 g) lightly crushed thick corn tortilla chips (about 6 ounces [170 g])
- Crumbled Mexican cheese
- Chopped fresh cilantro, for garnish
- Sour cream, for garnish

Preheat the grill to high heat. Season the chicken with salt and pepper. Place the chicken in a resealable plastic bag and add garlic, oregano, 2 tablespoons (38 ml) of tequila, and 2 tablespoons (30 ml) olive oil. Close the bag, squeezing out the air. Rub the chicken in the marinade, coating each piece thoroughly. Marinate for at least 30 minutes. If longer, chill the chicken in its bag, marinating for at most 24 hours, removing from the refrigerator 10 minutes prior to cooking. Place the chicken on the hot grill and cook 5 to 7 minutes per side, until browned and the internal temperature on an instant-read thermometer registers 170°F (77°C). Transfer to a plate and cool. Shred the chicken and place in a bowl. In a 9 × 13-inch (23 × 33 cm) ovenproof baking dish, combine the remaining 1/4 cup (60 ml) of tequila, 2 tablespoons (30 ml) olive oil, and the cumin, chili powder, tomatoes, hominy, jalapeños, and corn. Add the tortilla chips, tossing to combine. Scatter chicken evenly over the tortilla chips. Top with cheese. Bake for 30 minutes; broil to brown the top, remove from the heat, and serve.

Prep = 1 hour including marinating
Cook = 40 minutes **Yield** = 4 to 6 servings

Breaded Chicken with Tarragon-Cognac Sauce

Butterflied, pounded chicken, as is used in this recipe, makes for a quick-cooking dish. Pound it yourself, or, alternatively, buy pounded chicken in the poultry section of most supermarkets or ask your butcher to pound boneless breasts for you.

6	(6-ounce [168 g]) boneless, skinless chicken breasts
2	cups (220 g) all-purpose flour
1	teaspoon freshly ground sea salt
1	teaspoon freshly ground black pepper
3	eggs, beaten with 1 tablespoon (15 ml) milk
1 1/2	cups (75 g) fresh bread crumbs
3	tablespoons (45 ml) extra-virgin olive oil
4	uncooked slices bacon, cut into 1/2-inch (1.3 cm) pieces
1	sweet yellow onion, chopped
3	cloves garlic, minced
12	ounces (340 g) baby cremini mushrooms, cleaned and sliced
1/2	cup (120 ml) cognac
1	(15-ounce [428 g]) can good-quality tomato sauce
1	cup (235 ml) chicken stock
2	tablespoons (8 g) minced fresh tarragon
1	tablespoon (4 g) minced fresh flat-leaf parsley

Butterfly the chicken breasts by laying them flat on a clean, dry cutting board. Working with a sharp boning or chef's knife, with the thickest end of the chicken facing you, slice the breasts in half horizontally being careful not to cut all the way through. Open up the breasts to resemble two butterfly wings. If necessary, cover with plastic wrap and pound lightly to make the breasts a consistent ¼-inch (6 mm) thickness. Set up a breading station for the chicken: In a pie plate or shallow dish, place the flour with the salt and pepper, stirring with a fork to combine. Place the eggs in another pie plate, and the bread crumbs in a third pie plate. Dredge a breast in the flour, coating evenly and thoroughly, then dip into the egg, and then into the bread crumbs, coating evenly. Set aside onto a sheet pan or tray. Repeat with each chicken breast.

In a large, deep sauté pan over medium heat, heat 1 tablespoon (15 ml) of the olive oil. Add the sliced bacon and cook until browned and crisp, about 5 minutes. Transfer the bacon to paper towels and set aside. In the same skillet, add the chicken breasts, as many as will fit in the pan without crowding, and brown on both sides. As they brown, transfer to a platter. Once all the chicken is browned, add the remaining 2 tablespoons (30 ml) oil to the pan. Add the onion and garlic and sauté for 1 minute. Add the mushrooms and sauté until tender, about 3 minutes. Deglaze the pan with the cognac, stirring to scrape up all the bits on the bottom of the skillet. Add the tomato sauce, chicken stock, and cooked bacon, stirring to combine. Cook for 2 minutes. Stir in the tarragon, add the chicken breasts back to the skillet, ladle sauce over each piece, and cook for an additional 10 minutes over low heat, until the chicken is cooked through. Sprinkle with the parsley and serve.

Prep = 20 minutes **Cook** = 30 minutes **Yield** = 6 servings

Kahlúa Chicken with Glazed Shallot and Leeks

As a rub or marinade, coffee has certainly found its place in the kitchen, but using coffee liqueur in a savory sauce is maybe a little less common. When reduced in the pan with butter, the Kahlúa and balsamic vinegar are a velvety, rich triumph.

MARINADE:

- ¼ cup (60 ml) coffee liqueur, such as Kahlúa
- 2 tablespoons (30 ml) balsamic vinegar
- 1 tablespoon (20 g) honey
- 1 tablespoon (15 ml) olive oil
- ½ teaspoon ancho chile powder
- ½ teaspoon chili powder
- 1 teaspoon freshly ground black pepper
- ½ teaspoon salt
- 1 teaspoon chopped fresh rosemary

CHICKEN:

- 2 (8-ounce) boneless, skinless chicken breasts
- 1 tablespoon (15 ml) extra-virgin olive oil
- 1 tablespoon (14 g) unsalted butter
- 1 shallot, peeled and thinly sliced
- 1 leek, pale and green parts only, washed well and thinly sliced
- 1 tablespoon (15 ml) coffee liqueur
- 1 tablespoon (15 ml) balsamic vinegar
- 1 cup (235 ml) chicken broth

For the marinade: Place the coffee liqueur, balsamic vinegar, honey, oil, ancho chile powder, chile powder, black pepper, salt, and rosemary, in a sealable container, whisking to combine.

For the chicken: Butterfly the chicken breasts by laying them flat on a clean, dry cutting board. Working with a sharp boning knife, with the thickest end of the chicken facing you, slice the breasts in half horizontally being careful not to cut all the way through. Open up the breasts to resemble two butterfly wings. If necessary, cover with plastic wrap and pound lightly to make the breasts a consistent thickness. Transfer the chicken to the marinade container, turning to coat. Cover and refrigerate for at least 30 minutes and up to 1 hour. Bring to room temperature before cooking. Heat the oil and butter in a large skillet over medium-high heat. Add the chicken to the skillet, browning for 7 minutes per side. Transfer to a plate and set aside. Add the shallot and leek to the pan and sauté until the shallot just begins to turn translucent, about 3 minutes. Add the coffee liqueur and vinegar, stirring to deglaze the pan. Stir in the chicken broth, bring to a boil, reduce heat and simmer for 3 minutes. Add the chicken back to the skillet with any juices, and cook for an additional 5 minutes, until cooked through, turning a few times in the pan. Serve topped with sauce.

Prep = 40 minutes including marinating **Cook** = 30 minutes
Yield = 4 servings

Prosciutto-Wrapped Chicken with Rosemary Vodka Pan Sauce

Using one of the homemade, flavored vodkas from pages 42 to 45, this chicken is a culinary delight. With restaurant-quality flavors but home-cooking ease, the dish comes together quickly but with plenty of flavor to delight.

4	(8-ounce [225 g]) boneless, skinless chicken breasts, washed and patted dry
	Salt and freshly ground black pepper
4	sprigs plus 1 teaspoon chopped fresh rosemary
8	thin slices good-quality prosciutto
3	tablespoons (45 ml) extra-virgin olive oil
2	shallots, minced
3	cloves garlic, minced
½	cup (75 g) seeded and diced tomato
½	cup (120 ml) Rosemary Vodka (page 44)
½	cup (120 ml) chicken broth
1	tablespoon (4 g) minced fresh flat-leaf parsley
3	tablespoons (42 g) unsalted butter, cold

Preheat oven to 400°F (200°C, or gas mark 6). Season the chicken breasts generously with salt and black pepper. Place a sprig of rosemary on each breast and wrap with 2 slices of prosciutto. Heat the olive oil in a large skillet over medium heat. Add the chicken and cook until golden, about 7 minutes per side. Transfer the chicken to a plate and set aside. Add the shallots and garlic to the pan and sauté until translucent, about 5 minutes. Add the tomato and cook for 3 minutes. Deglaze the pan with the vodka, stirring to scrape up any bits on the bottom of the skillet. Add the broth, parsley, and chopped rosemary, stirring to combine. Add the chicken back to the pan and roast for 15 minutes, until it has an internal temperature (check with an instant-read thermometer) of 170°F (77°C). Remove from the oven and transfer chicken to individual plates or a serving platter. Add the butter to the pan sauce 1 tablespoon (14 g) at a time, stirring into the sauce until melted and emulsified. Serve the chicken topped with the sauce.

Prep = 15 minutes **Cook** = 40 minutes **Yield** = 4 servings

Orange Chicken with Amaretto and Brie

Brie thickens this sauce, making it rich and creamy.

1 teaspoon freshly ground sea salt
1 teaspoon freshly ground black pepper
1 teaspoon paprika
4 (8-ounce [225 g]) boneless, skinless, chicken breasts, rinsed and patted dry
5 tablespoons (75 ml) extra-virgin olive oil
2 large shallots, halved and thinly sliced
1/2 cup (120 ml) amaretto liqueur
3/4 cup (175 ml) chicken stock
  Grated zest of 1 orange
1/4 cup (60 ml) heavy cream
6 ounces (168 g) Brie cheese, softened, rind cut away
1/4 cup (38 g) grated Pecorino-Romano cheese
2 tablespoons (8 g) roughly chopped fresh basil
1 (6-ounce [128 g]) bag arugula or baby spinach

In a small bowl, stir together the salt, pepper, and paprika. Butterfly the chicken breasts on a clean, dry cutting board. Working with a sharp boning knife, slice the breasts in half horizontally—do not cut all the way through. Open up the breasts to resemble two butterfly wings. If necessary, cover with plastic wrap and pound lightly to make the breasts a consistent thickness. Season each breast generously with the paprika mixture. In a large skillet, heat 3 tablespoons (45 ml) of the olive oil over medium-high heat. Add the chicken, browning on both sides, about 5 minutes per side. Transfer to a plate. Add the remaining 2 tablespoons (30 ml) olive oil to the skillet. Add the shallots and sauté for 3 minutes, until tender and turning golden. Add the amaretto, being careful of the rising steam, and stir to deglaze the pan, scraping up any bits from the bottom of the skillet. Add the chicken stock and orange zest and cook for 5 minutes to thicken. Add the cream, Brie, Pecorino-Romano cheese, and basil, stirring until Brie is melted and sauce is thickened. Add the arugula and cook, stirring, to just wilt and combine. Add the chicken and any juices back to the skillet and cook, turning in sauce, for 5 minutes, until the chicken is cooked through. Serve chicken over pasta or rice, topped with the sauce.

Prep = 15 minutes **Cook** = 30 minutes **Yield** = 4 servings

Bourbon-Brined Chicken

Brining the chicken in bourbon and tea is half the story; grilling it in bourbon finishes the dish.

4 each chicken halves (breast and leg sections), washed and patted dry, skin on

BRINING LIQUID:

2 cups (475 ml) bourbon
3 cups (710 ml) brewed tea
1 tablespoon (5 g) cracked coriander seeds
1 teaspoon peppercorns
½ cup (100 g) granulated sugar
½ cup (150 g) kosher salt
   Juice of 1 lemon
4 bay leaves
4 sprigs fresh thyme

GRILLING SAUCE:

¼ cup (60 ml) bourbon
¼ cup (60 ml) lemon juice
1 tablespoon (10 g) minced garlic
1 tablespoon (4 g) minced fresh thyme
2 tablespoons (30 ml) extra-virgin olive oil
1 tablespoon (13 g) granulated sugar
   Freshly ground sea salt and black pepper

Place the chicken in a large brining bag, or in a stockpot large enough to hold the chicken in the brine. Combine the bourbon, tea, coriander, peppercorns, sugar, and salt. Bring to a boil and stir until the sugar is dissolved. Remove from the heat, add the lemon juice, bay leaves, and thyme. Let the brine cool to room temperature, then add the chicken or pour the brine over the chicken in the brining bag. Cover and refrigerate for 4 hours. Remove the chicken from the brine and pat dry, and let come to room temperature. Preheat grill to high heat.

For the grilling sauce: In a small bowl, combine all the sauce ingredients. Baste the chicken with sauce. Season with sea salt and black pepper. Place the chicken on the grill and cook for 8 minutes per side, turning and basting several times during cooking. Transfer to a plate to rest for 5 minutes. Serve.

Prep = 15 minutes **Chill** = 4 hours **Cook** = 20 minutes
Yield = 4 servings

Chicken with Lemon Vodka and Capers

Here, citrus vodka provides a depth of lemon that benefits the dish. Good-quality vodkas provide a more natural lemon taste than do some of the lesser-quality ones, simply because the better brands typically use the extract of natural fruits.

1	lemon, sliced thinly
2	tablespoons (30 ml) extra-virgin olive oil
4	large boneless, skinless chicken breasts, rinsed and patted dry
	Salt and freshly ground black pepper
1/3	cup (80 ml) lemon-flavored vodka
5	tablespoons (70 g) unsalted butter
2	tablespoons (30 ml) freshly squeezed lemon juice
1	tablespoon (4 g) chopped fresh flat-leaf parsley
1	tablespoon (4 g) chopped fresh basil
1/4	cup (34 g) capers

Heat a small amount of the olive oil in a large skillet over medium-high heat. Char the lemon slices on one side in the hot oil, until just browned. Transfer to a plate and set aside. Season the chicken breasts with salt and pepper. Add the remaining olive oil to the pan. Add the chicken to the pan and cook until browned and cooked through, 5 to 7 minutes per side. Transfer to a plate. Deglaze the skillet with the vodka, scraping up all the bits off of the bottom of the pan. Add the butter, whisking to combine, then the lemon juice, parsley, basil, and capers, stirring to combine. Season with salt and black pepper and let reduce and thicken for 5 minutes. Add the chicken and lemon slices back to the pan, tossing in the sauce. Serve the chicken breasts with pasta or rice, topped with the sauce.

Prep = 10 minutes **Cook** = 20 minutes
Yield = 4 servings

Margarita Chicken Wings

Salt, lime, and tequila seem perfect flavors for spicy chicken wings. Serve these with a cold Margarita for a perfect summer treat.

4	pounds (1.8 kg) chicken wings, divided into two sections, wing tips discarded
1	cup (235 ml) añejo tequila
1/2	cup (120 ml) freshly squeezed orange juice
1/4	cup (80 g) honey
	Grated zest and juice of 2 limes
3	cloves garlic, minced
1	teaspoon ground cumin
1	teaspoon chili powder
1 1/2	teaspoons freshly ground black pepper
1	teaspoon freshly ground sea salt
1/4	cup (15 g) chopped fresh cilantro
2	quarts (1.9 L) vegetable or canola oil, for frying
	Honey Lime Dipping Sauce (page 30)

Wash and pat dry the wings and place in a large bowl. In a small bowl, combine the tequila, orange juice, honey, lime zest and juice, garlic, cumin, chili powder, black pepper, salt, and cilantro. Pour the marinade over the wings, tossing to coat evenly. Cover with plastic wrap and refrigerate for at least 2 hours or up to overnight. Preheat the oil in a large stockpot to 375°F (190°C). Preheat oven to 400°F (200°C, or gas mark 6). Drain the wings and pat dry. Place the wings gently in the hot oil and fry in batches until crispy and dark brown, 2 to 3 minutes (avoid overcrowding the pan). Place the wings back in the bowl of marinade, tossing to coat. Transfer to a sheet pan coated with nonstick cooking spray. Once all the wings are fried, place in the oven and bake for 30 minutes. Remove, let stand for 5 minutes, and serve with the dipping sauce. Alternatively, marinate the wings for the instructed time. Omit the frying and baking, and simply grill on high heat or broil, turning several times, for 20 minutes. Serve with the dipping sauce.

Prep = 15 minutes **Chill** = 2 hours **Cook** = 25 to 40 minutes
Yield = 4 to 6 servings

Fish and Shellfish

Salmon Gravlax

Salt and sugar are the real workers in this dish, but the spirit adds the needed moisture and a hint of spice that benefit the end result. Gravlax is most commonly used on bagels or toast for breakfast or brunch, but in salads and sauces, it is a flavorful addition to many dishes.

2	equal-size center-cut salmon fillets (about 3 pounds [1.4 kg] each), skin on, bones removed
1	cup (200 g) granulated sugar
1	cup (300 g) coarse sea salt or kosher salt
2	tablespoons (12 g) cracked black pepper
2	tablespoons (12 g) cracked coriander seeds
1	tablespoon (6 g) cracked fennel seeds
¼	cup (60 ml) gin
½	large bunch fresh dill, stems and leaves, coarsely chopped

Spread plastic wrap on a large sheet pan. Lay the salmon fillets flat on the plastic, skin side down, tails facing the same direction. In a bowl, combine the sugar, salt, black pepper, coriander, and fennel seeds. Cover each fillet evenly with the salt mixture. Sprinkle each fillet evenly with the gin. Cover one fillet evenly with the dill, then cover with the other fillet, tails aligning. Press the fillets together and wrap tightly with plastic wrap. Wrap the sheet pan tightly with plastic wrap. Place another sheet pan of the same size bottom down, on top of the fillets, and weight with heavy bricks or a pot to press the salmon evenly. Place in the refrigerator for 3 days, turning every 24 hours. After 3 days, remove gravlax, slice very thin slices from the skin, and serve with bagels and their accompaniments, or as a topping for salad or in a pasta dish. Serve with sliced fresh bagels, cream cheese, capers, thinly sliced tomato, thinly sliced red onion, and diced hard-boiled eggs.

Prep = 15 minutes **Chill** = 3 days
Yield = 3 pounds (1.4 kg)

Shrimp with Black-Eyed Peas

Traditionally served on New Year's Day, black-eyed peas bring good luck and prosperity.

BLACK-EYED PEAS:

- 2 tablespoons (30 ml) olive oil
- 4 uncooked slices bacon, chopped
- 1 sweet yellow onion, chopped finely
- 1 medium carrot, peeled and finely chopped
- 1 stalk celery, finely chopped
- 1/2 medium green bell pepper, seeded and chopped
- 3 cloves garlic, minced
- 2 bay leaves
- 1 jalapeño pepper, minced
- 2 (15-ounce [428 g]) cans black-eyed peas, rinsed and drained
- 3/4 cup (175 ml) sour mash whiskey
- 1 cup (235 ml) chicken broth

SHRIMP:

- 3 tablespoons (45 ml) olive oil
- 1 pound (455 g) large shrimp, peeled and de-veined
- 3 cloves garlic, minced
- 1/2 teaspoon freshly ground sea salt
- 1 teaspoon freshly ground black pepper
- 1/2 cup (120 ml) sour mash whiskey
- 2 tablespoons (28 g) cold unsalted butter

For the black-eyed peas: In a large skillet, heat the olive oil over medium-high heat. Add the bacon, cooking until it begins to turn golden, about 3 minutes. Add the onion, carrot, celery, and bell pepper and sauté for 3 minutes, until tender. Add the garlic, bay leaves, and jalapeño and sauté for 2 minutes. Add the black-eyed peas and cook for 4 minutes, then deglaze the pan with the whiskey, cooking for 2 minutes. Add the broth and reduce by half. Discard bay leaves.

For the shrimp: In a large skillet, heat the olive oil over medium-high heat. Add the shrimp and garlic and sauté for about 4 minutes. Season with salt and pepper, add the whiskey, stirring to remove any bits from the bottom of the pan. Add the butter, stirring to create an emulsion. Serve the shrimp over the black-eyed peas.

Prep = 20 minutes **Cook** = 25 minutes **Yield** = 4 servings

Mahi Mahi with Anchovy Tomatoes

Here, sweet, fleshy mahi mahi is paired with the bracing saltiness of anchovies, and spiced with both pepper-flavored vodka and vodka-flavored tomatoes, sending this Hawaiian fish in a whole new, exotic flavor direction.

4   (8-ounce [225 g]) mahi mahi fillets
    Salt and freshly ground black pepper
¼   cup (60 ml) plus 1 tablespoon (15 ml) extra-virgin olive oil
4   cloves garlic minced
1   large shallot, minced
4   anchovy fillets
¼   cup (60 ml) pepper-flavored vodka
1   (14-ounce [400 g]) can crushed tomatoes
2   tablespoons (9 g) chopped Oven Dried Balsamic-Vodka Tomatoes (page 168) or sun-dried tomatoes
1   teaspoon dried oregano
1   tablespoon (4 g) chopped fresh flat-leaf parsley
1   tablespoon (4 g) chopped fresh basil

Season the mahi mahi generously with salt and pepper. Heat ¼ cup (60 ml) of the olive oil in a large skillet over medium-high heat. Add the mahi mahi and brown on both sides, about 5 minutes per side; transfer to a plate. Add the remaining 1 tablespoon (15 ml) of oil to the pan and heat. Add the garlic and shallot and sauté just until tender, about 2 minutes. Add the anchovy fillets, cooking until basically dissolved, about 3 minutes. Deglaze the pan with the vodka, stirring for 2 minutes. Add the crushed tomatoes, oven-dried tomatoes, and herbs, stirring to combine. Add the fish back to the skillet, spooning the sauce over them. Cook for an additional 5 minutes, or until the fish begins to flake when pierced with a fork. Serve the fish topped with the sauce.

Prep = 15 minutes   **Cook** = 25 minutes   **Yield** = 4 servings

Fennel Crab with Gnocchi and Anisette

Yet another variation on an anise-based flavor pairs anisette liqueur and fennel seeds with sweet crabmeat. The truffle oil adds an earthy touch.

- 1 pound (455 g) fresh or frozen gnocchi
- 2 tablespoons (30 ml) olive oil
- 2 tablespoons (28 g) butter
- 1 teaspoon truffle oil
- 1/2 red onion, thinly sliced
- 1 shallot, thinly sliced
- 3 cloves garlic, minced
- 1 pound (455 g) thick asparagus, ends trimmed, sliced lengthwise into thin strips
- 8 ounces (225 g) lump crabmeat, picked over for any shells
- 1/2 teaspoon freshly ground sea salt
- 1/2 teaspoon freshly ground black pepper
- 1 teaspoon ground fennel seeds,
- 1 tablespoon (15 ml) anisette liqueur
- 1/2 cup (120 ml) chicken broth
- 1/4 cup (60 ml) heavy cream

Cook the gnocchi in a pot of boiling salted water until tender, about 5 minutes for fresh and 9 minutes for frozen. Drain, run under cold water to cool, and set aside. In a large skillet, heat the olive oil, butter, and truffle oil over medium-high heat. Add the red onion and sauté for 2 minutes. Add the shallot, garlic, and asparagus and sauté until tender and the shallot begins to turn golden. Add the crabmeat and cook for 2 minutes. Season with salt, pepper, and fennel seeds, stirring to combine. Deglaze the pan with the anisette and chicken broth, stirring to scrape up any browned bits on the bottom of the pan. Bring to a boil and let the liquid reduce for 2 minutes. Add the heavy cream, bring to a boil again, and cook for 2 additional minutes. Stir in the cooked gnocchi, coating them well with the sauce, and serve hot.

Prep = 15 minutes **Cook** = 15 to 20 minutes **Yield** = 4 servings

Greek Fish Stew with Ouzo and Fennel

Ouzo joins fresh fennel and tarragon for a triple-header of licorice-like flavor.

- 1/3 cup (80 ml) olive oil
- 1 large yellow onion, diced
- 1 leek, pale green and white parts only, well washed, split in half lengthwise, and thinly sliced
- 1 large bulb fennel, quartered and thinly sliced
- 4 cloves garlic, minced
- 1 (14 1/2-ounce [412 g]) can diced tomatoes
- 2 bay leaves
- 3 sprigs fresh flat-leaf parsley
- 2 sprigs fresh thyme
- 1 cup (235 ml) white wine
- 1/2 cup (120 ml) ouzo
- 4 cups (950 ml) fish stock
- 1/4 teaspoon dried saffron threads
- 1 1/2 teaspoons sea salt
- 1 pound (455 g) medium shrimp, shelled and deveined
- 1 pound (455 g) sea scallops, cleaned
- 2 pounds (910 g) meaty white fish, such as cod, halibut, or monkfish, cut into chunks
- 1 pound (455 g) mussels, cleaned and debearded
- 2 teaspoons (28 ml) lemon juice
- 1 tablespoon (4 g) chopped fresh tarragon, for garnish
- 3 tablespoons (12 g) fresh parsley, chopped, for garnish

Heat the olive oil in a large casserole or braising pan over medium-high heat, add the onion, leek, and fennel, and sauté until tender, about 7 minutes. Add the garlic and cook for 3 minutes. Add the tomatoes, bay leaves, and parsley and thyme sprigs, and stir to combine. Stir in the white wine and ouzo and cook for 3 minutes. Add the fish stock, saffron, and sea salt and stir to combine. Add the shrimp, scallops, and fish and cook until the shrimp begins to turn slightly pink; at that point add the mussels and lemon juice and cover. Cook for 7 minutes, until the mussels are open. Discard bay leaves and any mussels that fail to open. Garnish the mixture with chopped parsley and tarragon and serve.

Prep = 30 minutes **Cook** = 30 minutes **Yield** = 6 to 8 servings

Sambuca Shrimp with Linguine

Sambuca, which originated in Civitavecchia more than 130 years ago, has a very distinctive flavor that, when used in moderation, can really enhance a dish. Here, it is a subtle but delicious part of this quick-to-prepare shrimp and pasta combination.

½ cup (120 ml) extra-virgin olive oil
3 cloves garlic, minced
2 shallots, minced
16 jumbo shrimp (13/15 size)
⅓ cup (80 ml) dry white wine
¼ cup (60 ml) sambuca liqueur
1 fresh tomato, seeded and diced
1 tablespoon (4 g) chopped fresh flat-leaf parsley
1 tablespoon (4 g) chopped fresh tarragon,
  plus extra whole leaves, for garnish
1 tablespoon (4 g) chopped fresh chives
1 teaspoon freshly ground sea salt
1 teaspoon freshly ground black pepper
8 tablespoons (1 stick, or 112 g) butter
1 pound (455 g) linguine pasta, cooked until al dente and drained
  Fresh Parmigiano-Reggiano cheese, for garnish

Heat the oil in a large sauté pan over medium-high heat. Add the garlic, shallots, and shrimp. Cook, stirring, for 2 minutes, until the shrimp just turns pink, then add the wine and sambuca. Hold the pan away from the burner and light with a match. Stir with a long-handled spoon or heatproof spatula until the flame has gone out and return to the burner. Add the tomato, parsley, chopped tarragon, chives, salt, and pepper and cook for an additional 3 minutes. Add the butter, lower the heat, and stir until the butter has melted. Cook for 3 minutes, allowing the juices to reduce. Pour the shrimp and sauce over four servings of the linguine. Garnish with freshly grated Parmigiano-Reggiano and whole tarragon leaves.

Prep = 20 minutes **Cook** = 15 minutes **Yield** = 4 servings

Tomato-Braised Cod

Basil is such a natural complement of tomatoes that most markets sell the herb right next to the fruit. But this recipe brings tomatoes to a whole new dimension with the addition of basil-flavored vodka.

4   (8-ounce [225 g]) fresh Atlantic or Pacific Cod fillets
     Freshly ground sea salt and black pepper
3   tablespoons (45 ml) extra-virgin olive oil
1   shallot, minced
2   cloves garlic, minced
1/2 cup (120 ml) Basil Vodka (page 43)
2   (14 1/2-ounce [412 g]) cans diced tomatoes
1/4 cup (15 g) fresh basil leaves, torn
2   teaspoons minced fresh chives
1/2 teaspoon red pepper flakes

Season the cod with salt and black pepper. Heat the olive oil in a large skillet over medium-high heat. Add the shallot and garlic and sauté until the shallot turns translucent, about 3 minutes. Add the cod to the pan and brown on both sides, about 5 minutes per side. Deglaze the pan with the basil vodka, scraping up any bits on the bottom of the skillet. Let cook for 3 minutes. Add the tomatoes, basil, chives, and red pepper flakes. Turn the fish a couple of times in the sauce while cooking for an additional 5 minutes. Serve the fish topped with the sauce.

Prep = 10 minutes **Cook** = 20 minutes **Yield** = 4 servings

Smoked Shrimp Gumbo

Not far from my grandmother's original, my gumbo features chorizo and dark rum, adding depth to the shrimp and okra.

- 7 cups (1.65 L) chicken stock
- 2 pounds (910 g) medium shrimp, shelled and deveined, shells reserved
- 4 tablespoons (½ stick, or 55 g) unsalted butter
- 8 ounces (225 g) chorizo, crumbled
- 1 large sweet yellow onion, diced
- 1 red bell pepper, seeded and diced
- 1 carrot, peeled and diced
- 2 cloves garlic, minced
- ¼ cup (28 g) all-purpose flour
- 1 teaspoon smoked paprika
- 1 cup (235 ml) well-aged, good-quality dark rum
- 1 (28-ounce [800 g]) can diced tomatoes, drained
  Salt and freshly ground black pepper
- 2 bay leaves
- 1 tablespoon (7 g) filé powder
- 1 (10-ounce [280 g]) package frozen okra, thawed, or 2 cups (200 g) chopped, fresh
- ½ teaspoon hot pepper sauce
- 8 cups (1.3 k) cooked rice

Place the chicken stock and shrimp shells in a large pot and bring to a boil. Lower the heat and simmer for 20 minutes. Strain the stock into a bowl and discard the shells. In a large Dutch oven, melt the butter, add the chorizo, and cook, stirring, for 5 minutes. Add the onion, bell pepper, carrot, and garlic and sauté for 10 minutes, until the onion is translucent and the carrot is tender. Sprinkle the vegetables with the flour and paprika and cook, stirring, for 7 minutes, until the flour has browned and is giving off a strong, nutty aroma; be careful not to burn it. Add the rum to the stock, then ladle the stock into the skillet, stirring to combine and prevent lumps. Repeat this until all of the stock is used. Add the diced tomatoes and season with salt and pepper. Add the bay leaves, filé powder, hot pepper sauce, and okra, stirring to combine. Bring to a boil, lower the heat and simmer for 30 minutes. Five minutes before the end of cooking time, add the shrimp, stir, and cook for the remaining 5 minutes. Serve over rice.

Prep = 20 minutes **Cook** = 1 hour and 15 minutes minutes
Yield = 8 servings

Halibut with Pineapple and Spiced Rum Chutney

This is an unusual sweet, sour, spicy turn for what can be a bland fish, uniting dried and fresh fruit, balsamic vinegar, and an all-important splash of spiced rum.

3   pounds (1.4 kg) fresh halibut steaks (six ½-pound [225 g] servings), skinned
    Freshly ground sea salt and black pepper
3   tablespoons (45 ml) olive oil
3   tablespoons (42 g) bacon grease or butter
⅓   cup (80 ml) spiced rum

CHUTNEY:
2   tablespoons (30 ml) olive oil
¾   cup (120 g) diced yellow onion
¼   cup (41 g) dried currants
2   cloves garlic, minced
1   yellow bell pepper, seeded and diced
1   (20-ounce [560 g]) can diced pineapple
1   cup (150 g) halved cherry or grape tomatoes
2   whole cloves
¼   cup (55 g) loosely packed light brown sugar
¼   cup (60 ml) plus 2 tablespoons (30 ml) white balsamic vinegar
¼   cup (60 ml) spiced rum
1   tablespoon (13 g) granulated sugar

Season each halibut steak generously with salt and black pepper. Heat the oil and bacon grease in a large skillet over medium-high heat. Place the halibut skinned side down in the skillet and cook for 7 minutes, moving the skillet periodically to loosen. Turn and cook for an additional 5 minutes. Deglaze the pan with the rum, swirling the pan around as you scrape up the bits on the bottom. Transfer the halibut to serving plates and continue cooking the glaze for 1 minute longer. Set aside.

Prep = 15 minutes **Cook** = 35 minutes **Yield** = 6 servings

For the chutney: Heat the olive oil in a saucepan over medium-high heat. Add the onion, currants, garlic, and yellow pepper and sauté until tender and the onion just begins to turn golden. Add the pineapple, tomatoes, cloves, brown sugar, and ¼ cup (60 ml) of balsamic vinegar, stir to combine, and cook for 20 minutes, until the sauce thickens. Strain the chutney, leaving the liquid behind in the saucepan. Discard the cloves. Keeping the pan over medium heat, add the spiced rum, remaining 2 tablespoons (30 ml) white balsamic vinegar and the granulated sugar. Cook the sauce, swirling the pan, until thickened, about 7 minutes. Remove from the heat. Serve the halibut with its glaze, the chutney, and the rum mixture from the second pan.

Mussels with Tomato Sambuca Broth

This is another terrific pairing of sambuca with seafood, in an eminently Mediterranean dish.

2	tablespoons (30 ml) extra-virgin olive oil
1	large yellow onion, diced
6	cloves garlic, minced
2	cups (475 ml) water
1	cup (235 ml) sambuca liqueur
1	(14½-ounce [412 g]) can diced tomatoes
3	pounds (1.4 kg) fresh mussels, cleaned and debearded
¼	cup (15 g) minced fresh basil
2	tablespoons (8 g) minced fresh flat-leaf parsley

In a large stockpot with a lid, heat the olive oil over high heat. Add the onion and garlic and sauté until the onion become tender, about 3 minutes. Add the water, sambuca, and tomatoes, stirring to combine. Add the mussels, cover, and let steam until all are opened, about 10 minutes. Discard any mussels that fail to open. Transfer the mussels with their broth to a serving bowl. Sprinkle with the basil and parsley and toss to combine. Serve with a warm crusty bread.

Prep = 20 minutes **Cook** = 15 minutes **Yield** = 4 servings

Mussels with Wheat Beer and Whiskey

One of my favorite ways to prepare mussels is in a rich and flavorful beer and whiskey broth. This recipe will feed about four people, but doubling it is just fine as long as you have a pot big enough to handle the mussels.

- 2 tablespoons (30 ml) olive oil
- 1 pound (455 g) chorizo (mild or hot), chopped
- 1 yellow onion, chopped
- 4 cloves garlic, chopped
- 1 yellow or red bell pepper, seeded and chopped
  Salt and freshly ground black pepper
- 1 (12-ounce [175 ml]) bottle German Hefeweizen-style beer
- ½ cup (120 ml) Irish whiskey
- 1 (14.5-ounce [412 g]) can diced tomatoes with juice
- 3 pounds (1.4 k) mussels, cleaned and debearded

Heat the oil over medium-high heat in a large stockpot with a lid. Add the chorizo and cook until just turning brown, about 5 minutes. Add the onion, garlic, and bell pepper and cook until tender, about 5 minutes, then season lightly with salt and black pepper. Add the beer, whiskey, and tomatoes and stir to combine. Add the mussels, cover the pot, and steam for 15 minutes, until all the mussels open. Discard any mussels that fail to open. Pour into a large serving bowl, ensuring that the sauce covers and drips down through the mussels. Serve with warm crusty bread for dipping.

Prep = 15 minutes **Cook** = 25 minutes **Yield** = 4 servings

St-Germain Poached Salmon over Mixed Greens

As varied as the flavors and ingredients of elderflower-based St-Germain are the flavors and textures of this elegant salad. A delicate poached salmon is the perfect way to feature such a liqueur because of its unique and subtle, sweet bite.

6	cups (1.4 L) water	
2 ½	cups (570 ml) St-Germain liqueur	
2	sprigs fresh flat-leaf parsley	
½	tablespoon (2.5 g) black peppercorns	
4	whole allspice berries	
3	bay leaves	
1 ½	pounds (685 g) salmon fillets, skinned, cut into 4 equal portions	

ST-GERMAIN VINAIGRETTE:

½	cup (120 ml) extra-virgin olive oil	
2	tablespoons (30 ml) St-Germain liqueur	
2	tablespoons (30 ml) white wine vinegar, such as sauvignon blanc	
2	tablespoons (30 ml) fresh lemon juice	
2	teaspoons minced fresh flat-leaf parsley	
	Freshly ground sea salt and black pepper	

1	tablespoon (15 ml) extra-virgin olive oil	
1	red onion, quartered and thinly sliced	
4	cups (80 g) mixed fresh salad greens	
4	red beets, roasted, peeled, and sliced	

In a large saucepan, combine the water, St-Germaine, parsley, peppercorns, allspice, and bay leaves. Bring to a boil over high heat. Gently add the salmon pieces and poach for 7 minutes. Transfer the salmon, draining over the pot, to a plate to cool.

For the vinaigrette: Combine all the ingredients for the vinaigrette in a sealable container or jar with a tight-fitting lid. Shake vigorously to combine, then refrigerate for at least 30 minutes (while the salmon cools).

In a small sauté pan, heat the olive oil over medium heat. Add the red onion and cook for 2 minutes, turning in the pan to keep it from browning. Decrease the heat to low and let the onion cook just until wilted and translucent, about 3 minutes, then transfer to a plate and set aside. Just before serving, toss the greens with a generous amount of the vinaigrette, then divide among 4 serving plates. Top each salad with the roasted beets, place a piece of salmon on top, and top with the wilted red onions. Sprinkle the salmon with additional vinaigrette, season with salt and black pepper, and serve.

Prep = 15 minutes   **Cook** = 15 minutes   **Chill** = 30 minutes
Yield = 4 servings

Shrimp with Olives and Lemon Vodka Sauce

At any tapas bar, you will find some small plate of shrimp and a bowl of assorted olives on the menu. Of course these go great with any cocktail, so why not skip a step and combine them in one pan with a delicate, sweet, and tangy lemon-flavored vodka.

1 pound (455 g) dried fettuccine
½ cup (120 ml) extra-virgin olive oil
1 lemon, thinly sliced
1 tablespoon (8.6 g) capers
3 shallots, minced
1½ cups (150 g) mixed olives
3 cloves garlic, minced
1 pound (455 g) large shrimp, peeled and deveined
½ cup (120 ml) lemon-flavored vodka
1 tablespoon (15 ml) lemon juice
3 tablespoons (42 g) butter
Salt and freshly ground pepper
1 tablespoon (4 g) chopped fresh basil

In a large pot of boiling salted water, cook the fettucccine until al dente, about 9 minutes, then drain and set aside. Heat the olive oil in a large skillet over medium-high heat. Add the lemon slices and brown on one side, about 5 minutes, and transfer to a plate. Add the capers to the same skillet, frying in the oil until popped open and fragrant, about 5 minutes, transfer to a plate. In the same skillet, add the shallots and olives and cook, stirring, until the olives begin to shrivel and the shallots start to brown, about 7 minutes. Add the garlic and cook for 3 minutes. Add the shrimp and cook until they begin to turn pink, about 5 minutes, stirring constantly. Deglaze the pan with the vodka and lemon juice, stirring to combine, and scrape up any bits on the bottom of the pan. Add the capers back to the pan, stirring to combine. Stir in the butter 1 tablespoon (14 g) at a time until melted and emulsified with the sauce. Season with salt and black pepper, stir in the basil, garnish with lemon slices, and serve over the fettuccine.

Prep = 15 minutes **Cook** = 40 minutes **Yield** = 4 servings

6

Meat

Whiskey Pot Roast

Loaded with the robust flavor of sour mash whiskey, plenty of vegetables, and garden-fresh herbs, this roast is delicious and warming. Put your slow cooker on overnight and wake to a delicious meal.

3	pounds (1.4 kg) bottom round roast, trimmed of excess fat
	Salt and freshly ground black pepper
3	tablespoons (45 ml) olive oil
1	large sweet yellow onion, diced
6	cloves garlic, coarsely chopped
3	large carrots, peeled and cut into 1 1/2-inch (4 cm) pieces
10	ounces (280 g) cremini mushrooms, quartered
1	cup (235 ml) sour mash whiskey
3	tablespoons (45 ml) Worcestershire sauce
1	teaspoon hot pepper sauce, such as Tabasco
1/4	cup (75 g) barbecue sauce
2	tablespoons (32 g) tomato paste
1/2	pound (225 g) Red Bliss potatoes, quartered
2	bay leaves
3	sprigs fresh flat-leaf parsley
3	sprigs fresh thyme
2	cups (475 ml) beef broth
1	(14 1/2-ounce [412 g]) can peeled plum or whole tomatoes

Generously season the roast with salt and pepper on all sides. Heat the olive oil over medium-high heat in a large, deep skillet or Dutch oven. Add the beef, browning on all sides, about 3 minutes per side. Transfer the roast to the bowl of a large slow cooker. To the skillet add the onion, garlic, and carrots and cook for 5 minutes, just until the onion begins to brown, stirring constantly. Add the mushrooms and cook, stirring, for 2 minutes. Add the whiskey to deglaze the pan, scraping up all the bits on the bottom of the pan. Cook for 2 minutes, then add the Worcestershire sauce, hot pepper sauce, barbecue sauce, and tomato paste, stirring to combine. Cook for 3 minutes. To the slow cooker, add the potatoes, herbs, and beef broth. Pour in the tomatoes, crushing as you do. Pour the whiskey and vegetable sauce over the meat. Cover the slow cooker and cook, according to the manufacturer's directions, on high for 2 hours. Turn the heat to low and cook for an additional 7 hours, or until the meat is fork-tender. Serve hot. Discard bay leaves and thyme sprigs.

Prep = 20 minutes **Cook** = 9 hours and 30 minutes
Yield = 4 to 6 servings

Beef Tenderloin with Cognac Peppercorn Sauce

With an intense flavor of spice, earth, leather, and honey, cognac is a tremendous spirit for cooking. Classic Cognac Peppercorn Sauce is the marriage of the peppercorn berry bursting in a bath of cognac and butter, thickened with a touch of cream … a perfect complement to traditional pepper-coated beef tenderloin.

- 6 tablespoons (90 ml) cognac
- 4 thick-cut beef tenderloin steaks
- 6 tablespoons (30 g) green or black peppercorns, lightly crushed
  Freshly ground sea salt (grind coarsely)
- 4 tablespoons (½ stick, or 55 g) cold unsalted butter
- ⅔ cup (168 g) crème fraîche

Place the cognac in a shallow dish, add the steaks, and let soak for 3 minutes per side. Place the peppercorns in a shallow dish. Remove the steaks from the cognac, letting the excess liquid drain off. Press both sides of the steaks in the peppercorns lightly, to coat with the pepper. Season each side of steaks lightly with coarsely ground sea salt. Melt the butter in a large skillet, add the steaks, and brown for 4 minutes per side for medium-rare and 7 minutes per side for medium, longer for well done. Add the cognac, swirling in the pan and cooking for 2 minutes, turning the steaks once in the sauce. Transfer the steaks to a plate. Pour the crème fraîche into the skillet, stir, and bring to a boil, scraping the bottom of the pan to scrape up any bits. Season with additional salt if necessary. Serve the steaks topped with the pan sauce.

Prep = 8 minutes **Cook** = 15 minutes **Yield** = 4 servings

Pork Chops with Rum Soy Sauce

Pork chops are an underutilized, underappreciated meat. Less expensive than most cuts of other meats and poultry, they should be part of your weekly dinner plans. Bone-in thick cuts of pork have more flavor and allow for a juicier end result.

1	teaspoon salt
1	teaspoon freshly ground black pepper
1/2	teaspoon paprika
6	pork loin chops (about 1/2 pound [225 g] each)
3	tablespoons (45 ml) olive oil
1	medium yellow onion, finely chopped
1	stalk celery, very thinly sliced on the diagonal
2	tablespoons (30 ml) light rum
3	tablespoons (45 ml) soy sauce
1/2	cup (120 g) tomato ketchup
1	teaspoon minced fresh ginger
1	cup (235 ml) chicken stock
2	cups (330 g) cooked rice

Preheat the oven to 350°F (180°C, or gas mark 4). Combine the salt, pepper, and paprika. Season each pork chop lightly with the salt mixture. In a lidded ovenproof skillet large enough to hold the pork chops, heat 1 tablespoon (15 ml) of the olive oil over medium-high heat. Brown the chops on both sides, then transfer to a plate. Add the remaining 2 tablespoons (30 ml) oil to the skillet, add the onion and celery, and cook until tender, about 3 minutes. Deglaze the pan with the rum, scraping up any bits from the bottom of the pan. Add the soy sauce, ketchup, and ginger and cook, stirring, for 2 minutes. Stir in the stock. Add the pork back to the pan, cover, and place in the oven. Cook for 45 minutes, until an instant-read thermometer inserted into a chop registers at least 145°F (63°C). Remove from the oven and serve with rice.

Prep = 30 minutes **Cook** = 1 hour **Yield** = 6 servings

Pan-Fried Garlic Sirloin Tips with Whiskey Pan Sauce

A few dishes in particular that I enjoyed on a recent trip to Portugal were those whose main ingredients were essentially fried in olive oil and flavored with garlic. This recipe is even tastier with the generous addition of whiskey.

      2   tablespoons (14 g) all-purpose flour
   1 1/2   teaspoons chili powder
     1/4   teaspoon salt (freshly ground sea salt preferred)
   1 1/2   teaspoons freshly ground black pepper
   1 1/2   pounds (680 g) sirloin tip steak
     1/2   cup (120 ml) good-quality, extra-virgin olive oil
      6   cloves garlic, sliced
      1   large shallot, halved and thinly sliced
     3/4   cup (175 ml) whiskey or bourbon
      1   cup (235 ml) beef stock
      1   sprig fresh rosemary

In a small bowl, combine the flour, chili powder, salt, and black pepper, stirring with a fork to combine. Place the sirloin on a plate and dust both sides generously and evenly with the spice mixture. Heat the oil in a large, deep skillet over medium-high heat. Add the sirloin tips to the oil and brown on one side for 4 minutes. Turn the steaks and add the garlic and shallot, moving them around in the skillet to combine while the steaks brown for an additional 5 minutes and the shallots and garlic cook until tender and browned. Deglaze the pan with the whiskey, stirring to scrape up all the bits on the bottom of the skillet. Cook, allowing the whiskey to reduce, for 3 minutes. Add the stock, black pepper, and rosemary. Stir to combine. Cook for an additional 3 minutes, while the sauce reduces. Transfer the meat to a serving plate. Stir the sauce and let reduce until thickened, about 3 more minutes. Discard the rosemary sprig. Serve the steak tips topped with the sauce.

Prep = 10 minutes   **Cook** = 20 minutes   **Yield** = 4 servings

Beef Steaks in Blackberry Brandy Sauce

This recipe is adapted from a favorite venison dish of mine. Here I have used beef steaks, which are just as good as the original, paired with sweet, rich blackberry brandy. If you have it, and like the taste, substitute venison loin steaks for the tenderloin—you will enjoy the flavor.

- ½   cup (120 ml) Armagnac or other brandy
- 4   thick-cut beef tenderloin steaks, at room temperature
- 1   pint (300 g) fresh blackberries
- ½   teaspoon granulated sugar
- 1   tablespoon (15 ml) blackberry brandy
-     Freshly ground sea salt and black pepper
- ¼   cup (½ stick, or 55 g) unsalted butter
- ½   cup (120 ml) beef broth

Pour the Armagnac into a shallow dish and place the steaks in the Armagnac, letting soak for 3 minutes per side. Meanwhile, place the blackberries in a small bowl, add the sugar and blackberry brandy, and stir. Transfer the steaks to a plate, allowing the excess Armagnac to drain into the dish. Season each side of each steak generously with sea salt and black pepper. Heat the butter in a large skillet over medium heat. Add the steaks and cook for 4 to 7 minutes per side (depending on whether you wish them to be medium-rare to well done). Pour the reserved Armagnac drippings over the steaks, swirling the skillet to combine the juices. Turn the steaks once in the Armagnac. Transfer the steaks to a plate. Add the blackberries with their juices to the pan and, using a wooden spoon, stir to loosen the bits from the bottom of the pan. Add the beef broth and let boil and thicken for 5 minutes. Serve the steaks topped with the sauce.

Prep = 10 minutes **Cook** = 15 to 20 minutes **Yield** = 4 servings

Jalapeño Burgers with Tequila Onions and Queso Fresco

Here, tequila gives caramelized onions an unmatched richness. Give the alcohol a chance to cook off, then sweeten with a touch of sugar and a perfect hamburger topping is born. The burgers pack a bold flavor with the addition of garlic and jalapeño peppers, a perfect foil for the sweetness of the onions.

3 pounds (14 kg) lean ground beef
4 scallions, green and white parts, finely chopped
1/2 cup (75 g) seeded and finely chopped red bell pepper
2 cloves garlic, minced
2 fresh jalapeño peppers, seeded and minced
1/2 cup (58 g) dry bread crumbs
2 eggs
2 tablespoons (28 ml) añejo tequila
2 teaspoons salt
2 teaspoons freshly ground black pepper
1 tablespoon (7 g) ground cumin
6 ounces (170 g) queso fresco

CARAMELIZED ONIONS:
2 tablespoons (30 ml) olive oil
2 tablespoons (28 g) butter
2 large sweet onions, thinly sliced
1/2 cup (120 ml) añejo tequila
1 tablespoon (13 g) granulated sugar
1/2 teaspoon sea salt
1/2 teaspoon freshly ground black pepper

TO SERVE:
6 hamburger buns
Lettuce and sliced tomatoes
1 ripe avocado, peeled, seeded, and sliced

In a large mixing bowl, mix the beef, scallions, red pepper, garlic, jalapeño, bread crumbs, eggs, tequila, salt, black pepper, and cumin. Form into 6 patties. Preheat the grill to high. Spray each burger with nonstick cooking spray. Place the patties on the grill and cook for 5 to 7 minutes on each side, depending on whether you prefer medium-rare or well done. Top each patty with queso fresco during the last 2 minutes of cooking, to melt. Toast the hamburger buns.

For the caramelized onions: In a large skillet, heat the olive oil and butter over medium-high heat. Add the onions and sauté, stirring, for 3 minutes, then lower the heat to medium. Cook the onions until just beginning to turn golden. Deglaze the pan with the tequila and season with sugar, sea salt, and pepper. Cook for an additional 5 minutes, until well caramelized, set aside.

For serving: Serve with lettuce, tomato, avocado, and buns.

Prep = 30 minutes **Cook** = 20 to 30 minutes **Yield** = 6 servings

Grilled Double-Thick Rum-Brined Pork Chops

You may have to ask your butcher to cut double-thick pork chops. I like mine about 1½ inches (4 cm) thick.

BRINING LIQUID:

- ¼ cup (55 g) firmly packed brown sugar
- ¼ cup (75 g) sea or kosher salt
- 4 cups (950 ml) water
- 1 cup (235 ml) dark rum
- 1 teaspoon whole allspice, lightly crushed
- 1 teaspoon black peppercorns
- 2 bay leaves
- 3 sprigs fresh rosemary
- 2 tablespoons (30 ml) white balsamic vinegar
- 4 bone-in thick-cut pork chops

BASTING SAUCE:

- ¼ cup (60 ml) dark rum
- 2 tablespoons (28 g) packed light brown sugar
- Zest and juice of 1 orange
- 1 tablespoon (15 ml) white balsamic vinegar
- 1 teaspoon dry mustard
- Salt and freshly ground black pepper

For the brining liquid: In a saucepan, combine the sugar, salt, water, rum, allspice, peppercorns, bay leaves, rosemary, and balsamic vinegar and stir over medium heat until sugar is dissolved. Remove from heat and cool for 20 minutes. Place the pork chops in a sealable container and pour the brining liquid over them. Cover and refrigerate for 4 hours.

For the basting sauce: Combine all ingredients in a saucepan and bring to a boil, to melt the sugar. Transfer to a bowl and set aside. Preheat the grill to high heat and remove the pork chops from the brining liquid, pat dry, discard the liquid. Spray both sides of each chop with nonstick cooking spray and season with salt and black pepper. Brush each side of each chop with the basting sauce and place on the grill. Cook for 7 minutes per side, turning a couple of times and basting. Transfer to a plate and let rest for 5 minutes, then serve.

Prep = 30 minutes **Chill** = 4 hours **Cook** = 15 minutes
Yield = 4 servings

Roasted Pork Loin with Orange-Ginger Sauce and Fresh Herbs

Ginger liqueur is a sweet, flavorful liqueur. This marinade made with ginger and orange flavors has a hint of Asian taste as well as a garden freshness from the herbs. Pork loin always seems perfect for any dish with an Asian influence.

4 tablespoons (60 ml) extra-virgin olive oil
2 cloves garlic, coarsely chopped
1 tablespoon (7 g) dried lemon zest
1 (1 1/2-pounds [680 g]) boneless pork loin, trimmed of any excess fat, washed, and patted dry
   Salt and freshly ground black pepper
1/2 cup (120 ml) ginger liqueur
1 cup (235 ml) fresh orange juice
1/2 cup (120 ml) chicken stock
1 sprig fresh rosemary
1 sprig fresh oregano
2 tablespoons (8 g) chopped fresh flat-leaf parsley

In a small bowl, combine 2 tablespoons (30 ml) of the olive oil with the garlic and lemon zest. Season the pork loin well with salt and black pepper. Place in a large casserole dish and rub generously all over with the lemon zest mixture. Heat the remaining 2 tablespoons (30 ml) oil in a large skillet over medium-high heat. Add the pork, and brown on all sides, turning as needed, about 7 minutes per side. Transfer the pork to a plate and set aside. Deglaze the pan with the ginger liqueur, stirring well to get any bits off the bottom of the pan, and cook for 3 minutes. Add the orange juice, chicken stock, rosemary, oregano, and parsley, stirring to combine. Add the pork and any juices back to the pan, spooning the sauce over it as it cooks for an additional 10 minutes, turning in the pan periodically. Transfer to a cutting board and slice into serving pieces; serve with the sauce.

Prep = 15 minutes **Cook** = 35 minutes
Yield = 4 servings

Pork Tenderloin with Fruit Reduction

Pomegranate liqueur, while quite sweet, is great for sauces and dressings. As a lot of sweet things do, pomegranate liqueur mixes well with balsamic vinegar.

MARINADE:

- ½ cup (120 ml) balsamic vinegar
- ¼ cup (60 ml) pomegranate liqueur
- 1 tablespoon (4 g) herbes de Provence
- ½ teaspoon freshly ground black pepper
- 3 tablespoons (45 g) olive oil

- 1 (1-pound [455 g]) pork tenderloin, trimmed
- ½ cup (75 g) dried sweet cherries
- ¼ cup (60 ml) pomegranate liqueur
- ½ cup (120 ml) brandy
- 2 tablespoons (30 ml) olive oil
- 10 ounces (280 g) cremini mushrooms, sliced
- ¼ cup (60 ml) balsamic vinegar
- 1 tablespoon (20 g) honey
- 2 tablespoons (28 g) unsalted butter
- 1 tablespoon (4 g) sliced cold sage leaves

For the marinade: In a bowl, combine all the ingredients for the marinade, whisking to combine. Place the tenderloin in a dish and cover with the marinade. Cover with plastic wrap and refrigerate for 1 hour.

Place the cherries in a bowl and cover with the pomegranate liqueur and brandy; set aside to soak for 30 minutes. Remove the pork from the refrigerator and let sit for 10 minutes. Slice the tenderloin into 1-inch (2.5 cm) -thick medallions. In a skillet, heat the olive oil over medium-high heat. Add the medallions to the skillet, cooking for 5 minutes per side. Transfer the medallions to a plate. Add the mushrooms to the skillet and sauté for 3 minutes. Add the cherries with the liqueurs to deglaze the pan, scraping up any bits from the bottom. Add the vinegar and honey, stirring to combine. Reduce for 2 minutes. Add the butter, 1 tablespoon (14 g) at a time, stirring to thicken the sauce. Add the pork medallions to the skillet and sprinkle with the sage. Continue to cook for 5 minutes. Serve topped with the sauce.

Prep = 30 minutes **Chill** = 1 hour **Cook** = 20 minutes
Yield = 4 servings

Bourbon Sausage Meatballs

With the powerful flavor of bourbon and chorizo, these meatballs are simply delicious. Quick to make and easy to cook, they make a great weeknight dinner with sauce and pasta, or serve with sauce and melted provolone cheese for a succulent meatball sub.

1	pound (455 g) freshly ground pork
1/2	pound (225 g) ground chorizo
1/2	cup (65 g) finely chopped yellow onions
2	tablespoons (8 g) chopped fresh flat-leaf parsley
1	tablespoon (4 g) chopped fresh basil
1	teaspoon dried oregano
2	teaspoons minced fresh garlic
1	teaspoon fennel seeds, crushed
1/2	teaspoon hot pepper sauce
2	tablespoons (30 ml) bourbon
1	teaspoon ground cumin
1/2	teaspoon freshly ground black pepper
1/2	teaspoon salt

Preheat the broiler to high. Combine all the ingredients in a large bowl. Use your hands to work the ingredients together until well combined. Form into 1 1/2-inch (4 cm) -diameter meatballs. Place in one layer on a large baking sheet. (Use more than one baking sheet if necessary; do not overcrowd the meatballs.) Position an oven rack in the middle of the oven under the broiler. Brown the meatballs under the broiler on all sides, turning several times until cooked through. Serve hot with your favorite sauce or add to Vodka Tomato Sauce (page 164), cooking for 10 minutes to flavor the sauce.

Prep = 10 minutes   **Cook** = 15 minutes
Yield = about 4 dozen meatballs

Italian Braised Chuck Steak

Chuck steak is a cut of meat that gets better and more tender the longer it cooks. This recipe calls for 2 hours of cooking to achieve exactly that—a fork-tender, moist, and flavorful dish. This could be made in a large slow cooker as well.

Salt and freshly ground black pepper
- 1/2 teaspoon paprika
- 3 pounds (1.4 k) beef chuck shoulder steak
- 6 tablespoons (90 ml) extra-virgin olive oil
- 1 medium yellow onion, diced
- 1 red chile pepper, thinly sliced
- 1 green chile pepper, thinly sliced
- 4 cloves garlic, coarsely chopped
- 2 bay leaves
- 1 sprig fresh rosemary
- 1 tablespoon (4 g) fresh thyme, minced
- 1 tablespoon (4 g) dried oregano
- 1 cup (235 ml) brandy
- 3 tablespoons (45 g) tomato paste
- 1 (28-ounce [800 g]) can whole peeled tomatoes

Preheat oven to 325°F (170°C, or gas mark 3). In a small bowl, combine the salt, pepper, and the paprika. Season the shoulder steak on both sides with the paprika mixture. In a large braising pan, heat 3 tablespoons (45 ml) of the olive oil over medium-high heat. Brown the steak on both sides for about 5 minutes per side. Transfer the steak to a plate; set aside. Add the remaining olive oil to the pan and heat. Add the onion, red and green chile peppers, and garlic to the pan and sauté until the onion is translucent, about 5 minutes. Add the bay leaves, rosemary, thyme, and oregano and cook for an additional 2 minutes. Deglaze the pan with the brandy and cook, stirring, for 2 minutes. Add the tomato paste, stirring to incorporate. Add the tomatoes, crushing, stirring, and cooking for 5 minutes. Add the steak back to the pan, spooning some of the sauce over the top. Cover and place in the oven for 2 hours, until the steak is fork-tender. Discard bay leaves and rosemary sprig. Serve over simple risotto or with rice.

Prep = 15 minutes **Cook** = 1 1/2 hours
Yield = 4 servings

Rib-Eye Steaks with Cognac Sauce

Rib-eye steaks have an abundance of flavor because of the greater marbling or fat content. I salt my steaks prior to searing, using freshly ground sea salt that leaves a fine crunch and flavor to the steak.

4	thick-cut rib-eye steaks (about 1 ½ inches [4 cm] thick)
	Vegetable oil, for rubbing steaks, plus 1 tablespoon (15 ml)
	Freshly ground sea salt and black pepper
2	tablespoons (28 g) unsalted butter, plus 2 tablespoons (28 g) chilled and cut into tablespoon-size (14 g) pieces
2	shallots, finely chopped
½	cup (120 ml) cognac or brandy
1 ½	cups (350 ml) beef stock
1	tablespoon (1.7 g) minced fresh rosemary
1	teaspoon minced fresh thyme

Heat a cast-iron or stainless-steel skillet over high heat until hot, about 7 minutes. Generously rub the steaks with oil and season with salt and black pepper. Cook the steaks one at a time, searing on each side, about 5 minutes per side, for medium-rare; 6 minutes on the second side for medium. Transfer the steaks to a plate and keep warm. Lower the heat to medium and add 1 tablespoon (15 ml) more vegetable oil with 2 tablespoons (28 g) butter. Add the shallots and cook just until tender, about 2 minutes. Deglaze the pan with the cognac, then add the beef stock, stirring up any bits on the bottom of the skillet. Add the rosemary and thyme and cook to reduce the liquid by half. Stir in the chilled butter 1 tablespoon (14 g) at a time to thicken the sauce. Serve the steaks topped with the cognac sauce.

Prep = 15 minutes **Cook** = 15 minutes **Yield** = 4 servings

Whiskey Lamb Stew with Potato and Green Chile

Meat and potatoes are considered comfort food no matter how they are prepared. The lamb and whiskey are the key ingredients in this vibrant, flavorful stew, which is bursting with fresh tomatoes and green chiles. Finish with crumbled Manchego cheese and tortillas for a crunchy and creamy garnish.

- 1/2 cup (120 ml) olive oil
- 4 cloves fresh garlic, chopped
- 2 medium sweet yellow onions, chopped
- 2 fresh jalapeños, thinly sliced
- 1/2 teaspoon salt
- 1 tablespoon (6 g) freshly ground black pepper
- 1 tablespoon (5.4 g) dried oregano
- 1 tablespoon (7 g) ground cumin
- 1 teaspoon chili powder
- 1 pound (455 g) lamb stew meat, cut into 1/2-inch (1.2 cm) cubes
- 3 tablespoons (45 ml) Irish whiskey
- 2 pounds (905 g) small yellow potatoes, cubed
- 1/3 cup (20 g) chopped fresh cilantro
- 2 cups (100 ml) canned, chopped green chiles
- 2 cups (360 g) chopped fresh or canned tomatoes
- 2 quarts (1.9 L) beef broth
- 1/3 cup (50 g) crumbled Manchego cheese
- Crumbled corn tortilla chips

Heat the oil in a large stockpot over medium-high heat. Add the garlic, onions, and jalapeños and sauté for 5 minutes, until the onions are tender. Season with salt, pepper, oregano, cumin, and chili powder and cook for an additional 5 minutes. Add the lamb and cook for 10 minutes, turning to brown all sides. Add the whiskey and deglaze the pan, scraping up any bits. Add the potatoes and cilantro and cook, stirring occasionally, for 10 minutes. Add the green chiles and tomatoes, stir to combine, and cook for an additional 3 minutes. Add the beef broth, lower the heat, and simmer for 1 1/2 hours. Serve the stew topped with crumbled Manchego cheese and crumbled corn tortilla chips.

Prep = 15 minutes **Cook** = 2 hours **Yield** = 10 servings

Grilled Pork Chops with Leek and Calvados Pan Gravy

Calvados is an aged apple brandy that is typically from the French region of lower Normandy. It is a great addition to both sweet and savory sauces.

1/2	teaspoon freshly ground sea salt
1	teaspoon freshly ground black pepper
1/4	teaspoon ground allspice
1	tablespoon (2.4 g) minced fresh thyme
4	thick-cut bone-in pork chops
2	tablespoons (30 ml) olive oil
3	tablespoons (42 g) unsalted butter
2	Fuji or Gala apples, peeled, cored, and thinly sliced
1	leek, both green and white parts, sliced
2	shallots, finely chopped
3	tablespoons (24 g) all-purpose flour
1	cup (235 ml) Calvados
2	cups (475 ml) chicken broth
2	sprigs fresh rosemary
2	fresh bay leaves
1/4	cup (60 ml) heavy cream

In a small bowl or dish, stir together the salt, pepper, allspice, and thyme. Season each pork chop generously with the spice mixture and set aside. In a large skillet, heat the oil and butter over medium heat until the butter is melted. Add the pork chops in one even layer and brown, about 7 minutes per side. Transfer the pork chops to a plate. To the same skillet, add the apples, leeks, and shallots and cook until the apples begin to brown and the leeks wilt. Sprinkle with the flour and cook, stirring, for 2 minutes. Deglaze the pan with the Calvados, scraping up any bits on the bottom. Add the broth, rosemary, and bay leaves, stirring to combine. Return the pork chops to the skillet and cook until the sauce thickens and the pork chops have reached an internal temperature of 160°F (70°C). Stir in the heavy cream and cook for 2 minutes. Serve the pork chops topped with the pan gravy. Discard rosemary sprigs and bay leaves.

Prep = 15 minutes **Cook** = 20 to 25 minutes **Yield** = 4 servings

Ouzo Lamb Chops with Herbs

Several favorite flavorings for lamb combine in this Greek-inspired recipe. Rosemary, garlic, and ouzo could each stand alone, but they are amazing when used in tandem as both a marinade and a sauce.

FOR THE MARINADE:
- 1/2 cup (120 ml) extra-virgin olive oil
- 1/4 cup (60 ml) red wine vinegar
- 1/4 cup (60 ml) ouzo
- 6 cloves garlic, minced
- 2 tablespoons (35 g) chopped fresh rosemary leaves
- 1 teaspoon freshly ground black pepper
- 2 tablespoons (8 g) chopped fresh mint leaves
- 24 frenched lamb chops (about 5 pounds [2.8 k])

HERB SAUCE:
- 6 tablespoons (83 g) unsalted butter
- 1/4 cup (60 ml) extra-virgin olive oil
- 1/4 cup chopped (16 g) fresh parsley leaves
- 1/4 cup chopped (10 g) fresh sage leaves
- 2 tablespoons (3.5 g) fresh rosemary leaves
- 1/2 cup (120 ml) ouzo

In a large sealable container, combine the oil, vinegar, ouzo, garlic, rosemary, mint, and black pepper. Add the chops, turn to coat, cover, and let stand for 30 minutes. Preheat the grill to high. Grill the chops for 6 minutes per side; they should be a little pink on the inside.

For the herb sauce: In a large skillet, melt the butter with the oil, add the herbs, and pan-fry until beginning to crisp. Add the ouzo and reduce by half. Serve the grilled lamb chops topped with the herbed ouzo sauce.

Prep = 40 minutes **Cook** = 15 minutes **Yield** = 8 servings

Slow-Cooked Kahlúa Short Ribs

Coffee liqueur and cola bring out an amazing depth of flavor when combined with slow-cooked beef.

4	pounds (1.8 kg) beef short ribs
	Salt and freshly ground black pepper
3	tablespoons (45 ml) vegetable or canola oil
2	sweet yellow onions, diced
4	carrots, peeled and sliced
6	cloves garlic, sliced
1 1/2	cups (350 ml) coffee liqueur, such as Kahlúa
1/2	cup (120 ml) beef stock
1/2	cup (120 ml) flat cola
8	sprigs fresh flat-leaf parsley
2	sticks cinnamon
1	sprig fresh rosemary

Season the ribs thoroughly with salt and black pepper. Warm the oil in a large skillet over medium-high heat. Brown the ribs in batches on all sides. Transfer to a slow cooker. In the same skillet, add the onions, carrots, and garlic, cooking until just tender, about 3 minutes, then season with salt and black pepper and transfer to the slow cooker. Add the Kahlúa, beef stock, cola, parsley, cinnamon sticks, and rosemary. Cook according to the manufacturer's instructions until the meat is falling from the bone, about 6 hours. Serve hot with your favorite rice and vegetable. Discard the cinnamon sticks and rosemary sprig.

Prep = 15 minutes **Cook** = 6½ hour **Yield** = 8 servings

Steak and Cheese Sandwiches with Bourbon Onions

You won't believe the richness of this classic sandwich, which just a modest amount of bourbon can accomplish.

- 2 tablespoons (30 ml) extra-virgin olive oil
- 1 large sweet yellow onion, thinly sliced
- 1 tablespoon (13 g) granulated sugar
- 1/4 cup (60 ml) bourbon
- 2 pounds (910 g) shaved beef steak
  Salt and freshly ground black pepper
- 4 split hard rolls
- 1/3 cup (75 g) mayonnaise
- 8 slices white American cheese

Preheat the broiler to high. Heat the olive oil in a large skillet over medium-high heat. Add the onion, tossing in the oil to coat evenly, and cook for 1 minute. Lower the heat to medium, add the sugar, bourbon, salt, and pepper, and cook the onion, stirring periodically, until caramelized and golden brown, about 15 minutes. Transfer the onion to a plate. Return the skillet to medium-high heat and add the shaved steak, cooking until browned through, about 7 minutes. Open each of the rolls, place on a sheet pan, and toast under the broiler for a few minutes, until just browned. Let the rolls cool slightly and brush the insides of the rolls with the mayonnaise. Add equal portions of meat and onion to the rolls. Top each with 2 slices of cheese and place under the broiler to melt the cheese. Serve the sandwiches hot right out of the oven.

Prep = 5 minutes **Cook** = 25 minutes **Yield** = 4 large sandwiches

Pulled Pork Sandwiches

Triple-threat apple flavorings—cider vinegar, cider, and apple brandy—transport these pork sandwiches to an autumn orchard.

- 1 tablespoon (19 g) freshly ground sea salt
- 1 tablespoon (6 g) freshly ground black pepper
- 1 tablespoon (7 g) yellow mustard seeds
- 1 bone-in pork shoulder (about 5 pounds [2.3 kg])
- 3 tablespoons (45 ml) extra-virgin olive oil
- 3 yellow onions, thinly sliced
- 1 red bell pepper, seeded and minced
- 4 cloves garlic, minced
- ½ cup (120 ml) whiskey
- 1 cup (235 ml) apple brandy, such as Laird's Applejack or Calvados
- 2 bay leaves
- 1 bunch fresh thyme
- ½ cup (120 ml) apple cider
- ½ cup (120 ml) cider vinegar
- 1 recipe Dijon Whiskey Sauce (page 40)
- 12 hamburger/sandwich buns

Preheat oven to 300°F (150°C, or gas mark 2). In a small bowl, combine the salt, pepper, and mustard seeds. Rub the pork all over, thoroughly, with the seasoning. Heat the olive oil in a large roasting pan or Dutch oven over medium heat. Add the pork shoulder and brown on all sides, then transfer to a plate. Add the onions, bell pepper, and garlic to the pan and sauté just until the onions are tender, about 3 minutes. Add the whiskey, apple brandy, bay leaves, and thyme to the pan and cook, stirring, for 5 minutes. Remove from the heat. Place the seasoned pork in the pan on top of the vegetables. Add the cider and cider vinegar. Cover and roast for 3 hours, then uncover and roast for an additional hour, until the internal temperature reads 180°F (83°C) on an instant-read thermometer. Transfer the pork to a plate to cool, reserving the vegetables. Shred the pork from the bone, removing any fat. Place the pork in a bowl. Transfer the vegetables to the pork, being sure to drain off the excess juice. Add the sauce to the pork, tossing to coat. Stuff each bun with shredded pork and serve immediately.

Prep = 15 minutes **Cook** = 4 hours and 20 minutes
Yield = 12 sandwiches

7

Vegetables, Pastas, and Sides

Slow-Cooked Tomatoes with White Beans and Ouzo

Orzo and beans take on an entirely new dimension with the addition of a mixture of fresh herbs and the anise-like scent and flavor of ouzo.

1 pound (455 g) dried orzo
6 plum tomatoes, halved
   Extra-virgin olive oil, for drizzling
1 teaspoon freshly cracked sea salt
1 teaspoon freshly cracked black pepper
2 cloves garlic, minced
2 tablespoons (8 g) minced fresh flat-leaf parsley
1 tablespoon(4 g) minced fresh basil
1 teaspoon minced fresh lemon thyme
2 tablespoons (30 ml) fresh lemon juice
2 tablespoons (30 ml) ouzo
1 (14 ½-ounce [412 g]) can white beans, drained

Preheat the oven to 400°F (200°C, or gas mark 6). In a large pot of boiling salted water, cook the orzo until al dente, about 7 minutes. Drain, run under cold water, and set aside. Place the tomato halves on a sheet pan. Drizzle each with olive oil, season with salt and black pepper, and top with equal amounts of garlic. Place in the oven and bake for 1 hour, until the tomatoes are browned and beginning to shrivel. Transfer the tomatoes to a cooling rack to cool for 10 minutes. Chop the tomatoes and place in a bowl. Toss the tomatoes with the parsley, basil, thyme, lemon juice, ouzo, and beans. Add the mixture to the orzo and toss to combine, seasoning with additional salt and black pepper if needed. Cover and refrigerate for 30 minutes; serve cold over mixed greens. For a hearty salad, add 1 pound (455 g cooked and shredded chicken breast.

Prep = 10 minutes **Cook** = 1 hour and 10 minutes
Chill = 30 minutes **Yield** = 4 servings

Penne alla Vodka

Penne alla Vodka is the marriage of tart vodka and fresh herbs with the depth of tomato. For added herbal infusion use one of the infused vodkas on (pages 42–45) instead of plain. Tomato paste gives this simple and elegant dish its classic pink color.

1 pound (455 g) penne or ziti pasta
2 tablespoons (28 g) unsalted butter
2 tablespoons (30 ml) extra-virgin olive oil
1 cup (235 ml) heavy cream
¼ cup (60 g) tomato paste
⅓ cup (80 ml) vodka
2 tablespoons (30 ml) chicken stock
  Pinch of red pepper flakes
2 tablespoons (8 g) chiffonaded fresh basil
1 teaspoon salt
½ cup (50 g) grated Parmigiano-Reggiano cheese

In a pot of boiling salted water, cook the pasta until al dente, about 9 minutes. Drain, reserving 1 cup (235 ml) of cooking liquid, and set aside. In a saucepan over medium heat, melt the butter with the oil and heavy cream. In a small bowl, whisk together the tomato paste, vodka, and stock. Add the vodka mixture to the cream and season with red pepper flakes, basil, and salt. Heat until thickened. Add the pasta to the sauce, tossing to combine, add the cheese, and toss. Add a bit of the cooking liquid if necessary to loosen the sauce. Serve hot with crusty bread.

Prep = 10 minutes **Cook** = 15 minutes **Yield** = 4 servings

Sautéed Vegetables with Ouzo

Tarragon is one of my favorite herbs, with its delicate leaf and vibrant anise-like flavor. Combining summer vegetables with anise-flavored ouzo and tarragon is a perfect union. Serve this dish alongside fresh grilled fish or chicken.

3 tablespoons (45 ml) extra-virgin olive oil
1 yellow squash, halved, quartered, and sliced 1/4 inch (6 mm) thick
1 green zucchini, halved, quartered, and sliced 1/4 inch (6 mm) thick
1/2 red onion, chopped
1/2 green bell pepper, seeded and diced
1/2 yellow bell pepper, seeded and diced
3 cloves garlic, minced
1/2 cup (35 g) sliced cremini mushrooms
  Freshly ground sea salt and black pepper
1/4 cup (60 ml) ouzo
1 tablespoon (4 g) chopped fresh tarragon
1 teaspoon chopped fresh flat-leaf parsley

Heat the oil in a large sauté pan over medium heat. Add the squash, zucchini, onion, and bell peppers. Sauté until just turning brown, about 5 minutes. Add the garlic and mushrooms, season with salt and pepper, stir, and cook for 4 more minutes, just until the mushrooms are tender. Deglaze the pan with the ouzo, add the tarragon and parsley, stir to combine, and cook off the alcohol for 2 minutes. Adjust the seasoning with salt and pepper as needed and serve warm.

Prep = 10 minutes **Cook** = 12 minutes **Yield** = 4 servings

Italian Oven Fries with Sambuca Mayonnaise

Who says french fries need only be served with ketchup? The sambuca, lemon, and Dijon-touched mayonnaise and Italian seasonings illuminate the potatoes with a tasty Mediterranean sunset.

2 pounds (910 g) baking potatoes, peeled and cut into french fry strips

¼ cup (25 g) grated Romano cheese

1 tablespoon (4 g) dried Italian seasoning

1 tablespoon (4 g) chopped fresh flat-leaf parsley

3 tablespoons (42 g) cold unsalted butter

Salt and freshly ground black pepper

SAMBUCA MAYONNAISE:

½ cup (112 g) mayonnaise

1 tablespoon (15 ml) sambuca liqueur

1 teaspoon Dijon mustard

1 teaspoon fresh lemon juice

Preheat the oven to 400°F (200°C, or gas mark 6). Place the potato strips on an oiled baking sheet large enough to hold all in a single layer. Sprinkle with Romano cheese, Italian seasoning, and parsley, dot the fries with the small pieces of butter, and season with salt and black pepper. Bake for 40 to 50 minutes, until the fries are golden and crisp. Remove from the oven, let cool for a couple of minutes, and serve with the sambuca mayonnaise.

For the sambuca mayonnaise: Stir together all the ingredients in a small bowl, cover, and refrigerate for at least 30 minutes. Serve with the fries.

Prep = 15 minutes **Cook** = 40 to 50 minutes **Chill** = 30 minutes
Yield = 4 servings

Vodka Tomato Sauce

Having a staple tomato sauce is a must for any household. This one is packed with flavor that your family will not be able to get enough of. I use the basil-flavored vodka, but you can certainly substitute Rosemary Vodka (page 44) or the Tomato Vine Vodka (page 45) for an equally great-tasting sauce.

- 2 tablespoons (30 ml) extra-virgin olive oil
- 1/2 cup (80 g) finely chopped onion
- 6 cloves garlic, coarsely chopped
- 1/2 cup (120 ml) Basil Vodka (page 43)
- 2 tablespoons (30 ml) red wine vinegar
- 1 (20-ounce [560 g]) can crushed tomatoes
- 2 (15-ounce [428 g]) cans tomato sauce
- 2 tablespoons (8 g) chopped fresh parsley
- 1/4 cup (15 g) chopped fresh basil
- 1/2 teaspoon salt
- 1 teaspoon black pepper

Heat the olive oil in a large saucepan or stockpot over medium-high heat. Add the onion and sauté until just tender and turning translucent, about 3 minutes. Add the garlic and cook for 1 minute. Add the vodka and vinegar, stirring to combine. Add the crushed tomatoes, tomato sauce, herbs, salt, and black pepper. Stir to combine. Lower the heat to medium and cook the sauce, stirring occasionally, for 20 minutes. Serve hot over your favorite pasta with Bourbon Sausage Meatballs (page 148).

Prep = 15 minutes **Cook** = 30 minutes
Yield = about 6 cups (1.4 L)

Grilled Corn on the Cob with Tequila Lime Butter

For a simple side on a summer day, farm-fresh corn on the cob with tequila, lime, and butter is perfect. Grilling corn is a great way to almost caramelize the flavors. Just turn a few times during grilling and the corn will become a toasted brown on the outside of each kernel, with a tender, juicy bite.

> 1 teaspoon chili powder
> 1/2 teaspoon paprika
> 1/2 teaspoon salt
> 1/2 teaspoon freshly ground black pepper
> 6 ears fresh corn, shucked, strings removed
> 6 tablespoons (83 g) unsalted butter
> 4 cloves garlic, minced
> 1/4 cup (60 ml) tequila
> Juice of 1 lime

Preheat the grill to high. In a small bowl, combine the chili powder, paprika, salt, and black pepper. Place each ear of corn on a piece of aluminum foil large enough to be able to wrap the cob completely in it. Sprinkle each ear with the spice mixture, turning and coating evenly. Wrap the corn in the foil, folding the ends closed. Place on the grill and cook for 10 minutes, turning every 2 minutes. Meanwhile, in a small saucepan, melt the butter with the garlic, tequila, and lime juice. Cook until the garlic becomes aromatic and browned, about 8 minutes. Remove the corn for the grill, unwrap each ear, and place on a serving plate. Spoon the tequila butter over each ear of corn and serve hot.

Prep = 10 minutes **Cook** = 10 minutes **Yield** = 6 servings

Wild Mushroom and Hazelnut Risotto with Frangelico

Risotto is perfect as an appetizer or an entire meal. The addition of the popular hazelnut liqueur Frangelico gives an unmatched boldness and depth to the dish. I found that the earthiness of the mushrooms is a perfect marriage with the nutty Frangelico.

- 4 cups (950 ml) chicken or vegetable stock
- 8 tablespoons (1 stick, or 112 g) unsalted butter
- 1 tablespoon (15 ml) olive oil
- 8 shallots, minced
- 1 cup (70 g) thinly sliced shiitake mushrooms
- 1 cup (70 g) thinly sliced oyster mushrooms
- 2 cloves garlic, minced
- 1 ½ cups (277 g) uncooked Arborio rice
- ¼ cup (60 ml) Frangelico or hazelnut liqueur
- 1 teaspoon salt
- ½ teaspoon freshly ground black pepper
- ¼ cup (60 ml) light cream
- 1 ½ cups (150 g) grated Parmigiano-Reggiano cheese
- ½ cup (30 g) chopped fresh flat-leaf parsley
- ½ cup (63 g) chopped, toasted hazelnuts (reserve 1 tablespoon [8 g] for garnish)

Place the stock in a large saucepan, keeping it warm over low heat. In a large skillet, melt the butter with the olive oil over medium-high heat. Add the shallots, mushrooms, salt, and pepper, and sauté until the shallots are just tender, about 2 minutes. Add the garlic and cook for 1 minute. Add the rice and stir to coat all the grains evenly. Add a ladleful of stock and the Frangelico to the skillet, stirring until the liquid is completely absorbed. Add another ladleful of stock, stirring and cooking until completely absorbed. Continue this, one ladleful at a time, until the stock is all absorbed and the risotto is creamy but still with a bite to it, about 20 minutes. Stir in the light cream, cheese, parsley, and hazelnuts. Serve warm, garnished with the reserved hazelnuts.

Prep = 15 minutes **Cook** = 30 minutes **Yield** = 6 servings

Oven-Dried Balsamic-Vodka Tomatoes

These tomatoes can literally be left alone to roast with little supervision. It takes them a while to achieve greatness in the oven, but the result is a treat. I use these in sauces, on bruschetta, and in spreads and dips, or just eat them right off the pan.

15	equal-size red, yellow, and green plum tomatoes (if you can't find the varying colors, all red is fine)
³/₄	cup (175 ml) extra-virgin olive oil
¹/₂	cup (120 ml) vodka
3	tablespoons (45 ml) balsamic vinegar
3	tablespoons (12 g) minced fresh basil
1	teaspoon freshly ground black pepper
2	teaspoons freshly ground sea salt

Preheat the oven to 250°F (120°C, or gas mark ¹/₂). Slice each tomato in half lengthwise, laying the halves skin side down on a sheet pan. In a jar with a tight-fitting lid, combine the oil, vodka, vinegar, basil, pepper, and salt, secure the lid, and shake vigorously to combine. Brush each tomato slice with the oil mixture, coating well, using all of the mixture. Place the tomatoes on the center rack in the oven and bake for about 8 hours. The time will vary, depending on the size of the tomatoes. It is important to use tomatoes of equal size so they all cook evenly. Once dried (the tomatoes will be shriveled to about half their original size and still be somewhat moist, not crispy) remove from the oven and let cool, or use immediately. To store, place the tomatoes in a jar with a tight-fitting lid, cover with olive oil, secure the lid, and refrigerate. The tomatoes will keep, refrigerated, for several months in oil. Alternatively, place in a freezer bag or an airtight container and freeze.

Prep = 10 minutes **Cook** = 8 hours **Yield** = about 2 cups (100 g)

Roasted Asparagus with Limoncello Pancetta Reduction

Asparagus is classically paired with a lemony hollandaise sauce. By introducing Limoncello, this is a faster, simpler way to achieve a similar pairing, with a delightful difference in flavor.

2 pounds (910 g) thick, fresh asparagus, ends trimmed
1 medium sweet yellow onion, peeled, halved, and thinly sliced
3 tablespoons (45 ml) olive oil, plus more for drizzling
Salt and freshly ground black pepper
3 ounces (85 g) thick-sliced pancetta, diced
1/4 cup (60 ml) Limoncello
1/4 cup (60 ml) balsamic vinegar
1/2 teaspoon dried lemon zest
1/2 teaspoon granulated sugar
2 tablespoons (28 g) cold butter

Preheat the oven to 400°F (200°C, or gas mark 6). Place the asparagus and sliced onion on a sheet pan or roasting pan. Drizzle evenly with olive oil and season generously with salt and black pepper, toss to coat evenly, and spread into an even layer. Roast on the middle rack of the oven for 20 minutes, or until the asparagus is tender and the onion has begun to brown. Meanwhile, prepare the sauce. In a small saucepan, heat the remaining 3 tablespoons (45 ml) olive oil over medium-high heat. Add the pancetta, cooking and stirring until browned, about 5 minutes. Deglaze the pan with the Limoncello, scraping up any bits from the bottom of the pan. Add the balsamic vinegar, lemon zest, and sugar, stirring and letting the mixture reduce to a thick sauce, about 5 minutes. Add the butter 1 tablespoon (14 g) at a time, stirring vigorously around the pat of butter to combine or emulsify into the sauce. Repeat with the second tablespoon of butter, with the sauce off the heat. The addition of the butter will make the sauce thicker and velvety. Transfer the asparagus and onion to a serving platter and top with the Limoncello-pancetta reduction.

Prep = 10 minutes **Cook** = 20 minutes **Yield** = 4 servings

Canadian Club Mushrooms with Bacon

I created this tasty mushroom side dish to pair well with any grilled or roasted meat, fish, or poultry. For wild mushrooms, use your imagination; shop at your local gourmet market to find unique varieties of wild mushrooms, such as blue foot, chanterelle, oyster, and lobster mushrooms. Look for fresh, local mushrooms, especially in the fall.

- ¼ cup (60 ml) extra-virgin olive oil
- 4 slices thick-cut smoked bacon, chopped
- 4 cups (280 g) assorted chopped wild mushrooms (leave small button or cremini mushrooms whole, stems trimmed)
- 2 cloves garlic, minced
- 1 teaspoon chopped fresh thyme
- ¼ cup (60 ml) Canadian Club whiskey
- 1 teaspoon chopped fresh flat leaf parsley
- ¼ teaspoon ground sea salt
- ½ teaspoon coarsely ground black pepper

In a large skillet heat 2 tablespoons (30 ml) of the olive oil over medium-high heat. Add the bacon, cooking just until turning crisp around the edges, stirring often, about 5 minutes. Add the remaining 2 tablespoons (30 ml) olive oil to the skillet and heat. Add the mushrooms tossing to coat evenly with the oil, sauté, stirring often, until the mushrooms just become tender and begin to brown, about 10 minutes. Add the garlic and thyme, cooking for 2 minutes. Add the whiskey, stirring to deglaze the pan. Reduce heat to medium, and cook for 5 minutes to allow the whiskey to reduce. Stir in the parsley, salt, and pepper and serve warm.

Prep = 15 minutes   **Cook** = 25 minutes   **Yield** = 4 servings

Italian Sausage and Kale Pasta

Inspired by Italian Kale Soup, this pasta dish can be served with a fork and a spoon. It is so hearty, with large bites of sausage and kale, drenched in a delicious broth. The whiskey, which could be substituted with cognac or brandy, gives the soup a lovely depth of flavor, bringing out the flavor of the sausage—a hearty meal for any night of the week.

2	tablespoons (30 ml) olive oil
1/2	pound (228 g) cooked sweet or hot Italian sausage, cut into 1/4-inch (6 mm) thick pieces
1	yellow bell pepper, seeded and thinly sliced
1	teaspoon minced fresh thyme
3	cloves garlic, minced
1	(19-ounce [540 g]) can cannellini beans, drained
2	cups (110 g) chopped fresh kale, stems trimmed
1/3	cup (80 ml) whiskey
1/2	cup (120 ml) beef stock
2	tablespoons (8 g) chopped fresh flat-leaf parsley
	Freshly ground sea salt and black pepper
1	pound (455 g) penne pasta, cooked until al dente and drained
1/4	cup (25 g) shaved Parmigiano-Reggiano cheese

In a large skillet, heat the olive oil over medium-high heat. Add the sausage and yellow pepper, cooking and stirring until the pepper is tender, about 5 minutes. Add the thyme, garlic, and cannellini beans, cooking for 3 minutes, stirring. Add the kale, cooking until bright green and just wilted, about 4 minutes. Deglaze the pan with the whiskey, scraping any bits from the bottom of the pan. Add the beef stock, reduce heat to a simmer, and cook for 5 minutes. Stir in the parsley, season with salt and black pepper, and serve over warm pasta. Top with shaved Parmigiano-Reggiano cheese.

Prep = 15 minutes **Cook** = 20 minutes **Yield** = 4 to 6 servings

Sweet Potato and Spiced Rum Soufflé

A pleasant fall treat, sweet potatoes baked in a fluffy, tender, flavorful soufflé are a great way to warm the house and the heart. Instead of overwhelming the dish with spices, I depend on the flavor of spiced rum to enhance the soufflé while allowing the sweet potato to speak for itself.

2 ½	pounds (2.1 k) sweet potatoes, scrubbed
4	tablespoons (½ stick, or 55 g) butter
1	yellow onion, minced
1	leek, white and pale green parts, well washed and minced
3	tablespoons (21 g) all-purpose flour
½	cup (120 ml) spiced rum
1	cup (235 ml) milk
¼	teaspoon ground nutmeg
¼	teaspoon ground allspice
¼	teaspoon ground ginger
1	tablespoon (13 g) granulated sugar
1	tablespoon (20 g) honey
6	eggs, separated
1	cup (110 g) shredded Gruyère cheese
½	cup (50 g) grated Parmesan cheese
	Salt and freshly ground black pepper

Preheat the oven to 375°F (190°C, or gas mark 5). Roast the sweet potatoes until fork tender, about 30 minutes. Remove from the oven and let cool. Once cool enough to handle, skin the potatoes and place in a bowl. Using a potato masher, mash until smooth. In a small sauté pan, melt 3 tablespoons (41 g) of the butter over medium-high heat. Add the onion and leek and sauté until translucent and golden, about 7 minutes. Add the flour, stir to incorporate, and cook for 3 minutes, until the flour begins to brown. Add the spiced rum, stirring constantly to prevent lumps—be careful of the rising steam from the pan. Add the milk and continue to stir until creamy and smooth. Add the spices, salt, and pepper, sugar, and honey and stir to incorporate. Add the egg yolks one at a time, stirring to incorporate after each addition, until smooth and the sauce is thickened. Pour the mixture into the sweet potatoes, stirring to incorporate. Add the Gruyère cheese, stir, and set aside. In the bowl of a mixer fitted with the whisk attachment, beat the egg whites until stiff peaks form, about 5 minutes. Gently fold half of the egg whites into the potato mixture until well incorporated. Fold in the remaining egg whites until no more white streaks are visible. Butter the sides and bottom of a 2-quart (1.9 L) soufflé dish with the remaining 1 tablespoon (14 g) butter. Dust the bottom and sides of the dish with three-quarters of the grated Parmesan cheese. Spoon the potato mixture into the prepared dish. Dust the top with the remaining Parmesan. Place on the middle rack of the oven and bake until puffed and golden, about 45 minutes, until a toothpick inserted into the center comes out clean. Serve warm.

Prep = 1 hour **Cook** = 45 minutes **Yield** = 8 servings

Mashed Red Potatoes with Sambuca and Parsley

Mashed potatoes are a basic comfort food that any home cook should master. The delicate but pleasing flavor of these anise- and truffle-flavored mashed potatoes will be a hit in your home.

- 2 pounds (910 g) Red Bliss potatoes, quartered
- 6 tablespoons (83 g) unsalted butter
- 1/3 cup (80 ml) milk
- 1 teaspoon freshly ground black pepper
- 1/2 teaspoon truffle salt
- 2 teaspoons truffle oil
- 2 tablespoons (30 ml) sambuca liqueur
- 1 tablespoon (4 g) minced fresh chives
- 1 tablespoon (4 g) chopped fresh flat-leaf parsley

Place a large pot of water over high heat. Add the potatoes, making sure the water covers the potatoes by 2 to 3 inches (5 to 7.5 cm). Bring the water to a boil and cook the potatoes at a rapid boil until tender, about 15 minutes. Drain and return to the pot. Add the remaining ingredients and mash with a potato masher until creamy and all ingredients are incorporated. Serve hot.

Prep = 10 minutes **Cook** = 15 minutes **Yield** = 4 servings

Braised White Beans with Sausage and Pernod

Derived from star anise and other herbs and botanicals, Pernod has a creamier approach, and a longer finish than its counterparts, sambuca and ouzo. It pairs well with sausage and white beans. This dish is intended as a side but certainly can be a meal by itself.

5	tablespoons (75 ml) extra-virgin olive oil
4	links Italian sausage
1	large sweet yellow onion, halved and thinly sliced
1	bulb fennel, quartered and thinly sliced
4	cloves garlic, minced
1/2	cup (120 ml) Pernod
1	(14 1/2-ounce [412 g]) can diced tomatoes
2	(19-ounce [532 g]) cans white beans, drained
	Salt and freshly ground black pepper
10	ounces (280 g) baby spinach
1	tablespoon (4 g) chopped fresh flat-leaf parsley
1/4	cup (30 g) fresh basil leaves, torn

Preheat the oven to 400°F (200°C, or gas mark 6). Heat 2 tablespoons (30 ml) of the olive oil in a large braising pan over medium heat. Add the sausage links to the pan and cook until browned on all sides, about 15 minutes. Transfer to a cutting board. Once cool enough to handle, slice the sausages on the diagonal into 1/4-inch (6 mm) -thick slices. In the braising pan, add the onion and fennel and sauté until the onion is tender and translucent, about 5 minutes. Add the sliced sausage and garlic to the pan and cook for 2 minutes, stirring. Deglaze the pan with the Pernod, stirring to scrape up any bits from the bottom of the pan. Add the tomatoes and the beans, season with salt and black pepper, and stir. Transfer the pan to the oven and cook for 20 minutes. Meanwhile, sauté the spinach in the remaining 3 tablespoons (45 ml) oil over medium heat, seasoning with salt and black pepper. Transfer the spinach to a serving platter, remove the beans from the oven, toss with the parsley and basil, and serve over the spinach.

Prep = 10 minutes **Cook** = 45 minutes **Yield** = 8 servings

Spiked Mac and Cheese

Still good for kids (because the alcohol cooks off) this "adulterized" spiked version of a time-honored classic is packed with flavor. With the addition of two of my favorite cooking spirits, spiced rum and brandy, this mac and cheese has that restaurant-quality creaminess and richness that you always wonder how they achieve.

½	sweet yellow onion
2	whole cloves
1	bay leaf
3	cups (710 ml) whole milk
5	tablespoons (70 g) unsalted butter
3	ounces (85 g) ham hock, cubed
2	sprigs fresh thyme
¼	cup (28 g) all-purpose flour
¼	cup (60 ml) spiced rum
2	tablespoons (30 ml) brandy or cognac
1	cup (120 g) shredded sharp white cheddar cheese
1 ½	cups (170 g) shredded Monterey Jack cheese
¼	cup (25 g) grated Parmigiano-Reggiano cheese
⅛	teaspoon freshly ground nutmeg (optional)
½	teaspoon salt
1	teaspoon freshly ground black pepper
1	pound (455 g) dried macaroni, cooked until al dente and drained
½	cup (58 g) dry bread crumbs

Stud the onion half with the two cloves by sticking the smaller ends into the onion; do the same with the stem end of the bay leaf. In a saucepan over medium heat, combine the milk with the studded onion, bring to a simmer just until the milk begins to bubble, turn off the heat, and let stand, stirring if necessary to prevent the milk from burning on the bottom. Just before ready to use the milk, remove the onion. In a large ovenproof Dutch oven, melt 4 tablespoons (55 g) of the butter with the ham hock and thyme sprigs over medium heat, stirring constantly. Cook until the ham and butter begin to brown lightly, about 5 minutes. Remove the ham pieces, sprinkle the butter with the flour, stirring constantly, and cook until the flour is pale brown, about 3 minutes. Decrease the heat to low and gradually pour in the warmed milk, whisking constantly to combine smoothly with no lumps. Add the spiced rum and brandy, stirring with the whisk to combine, and cook for 5 minutes. Remove the thyme sprigs and add the cheeses, nutmeg, salt, and black pepper, stirring with a wooden spoon until the cheeses are melted and the mixture is smooth. Stir in the macaroni, tossing gently to coat evenly with the cheese mixture. In a small skillet, melt the remaining 1 tablespoon (14 g) butter over medium heat and add the bread crumbs, stirring to toast for 3 minutes. Sprinkle the toasted bread crumbs evenly over the macaroni and serve. To reheat, place the amount you would like to reheat with milk to loosen in a saucepan over medium heat. Heat until bubbling and the cheese is melted and stringy.

Prep = 20 minutes **Cook** = 30 minutes **Yield** = 10 servings

Inside-Out Ravioli with Vodka and Tomato Sauce

This is ravioli without the fuss of the dough. The inside of the ravioli is always the best anyway, right? Augment Tomato Vine Vodka with Vodka Tomato Sauce for a tremendous, flavorful dish.

1	cup (100 g) grated Parmigiano-Reggiano cheese
2	cups (500 g) ricotta cheese, drained
1	cup (110 g) all-purpose flour
3	tablespoons (45 ml) Tomato Vine Vodka (page 45)
3	tablespoons (12 g) chopped fresh flat-leaf parsley
1/4	teaspoon grated nutmeg
1	tablespoon (13 g) granulated sugar
1	tablespoon (14 g) butter, melted
	Salt and freshly ground black pepper
1	cup (64 g) fresh basil, torn into small pieces
3	cups (710 ml) Vodka Tomato Sauce (page 164)

In a large bowl, combine the cheeses, flour, vodka, parsley, nutmeg, sugar, and butter, stirring until smooth. Season generously with salt and black pepper, add most of the fresh basil (saving some for garnish), and stir to combine. Using tablespoons, form the cheese mixture into 1 1/2-inch (4 cm) -diameter balls. Place on a sheet pan and refrigerate for at least 30 minutes. Bring a large stockpot three-quarters full of salted water to a boil over high heat. Gently drop the chilled cheese balls into the boiling water and cook for 3 minutes, until just warmed through. Meanwhile, heat the tomato sauce in a saucepan. Place the warmed sauce on serving plates and top with the cooked cheese. Season with fresh cracked pepper, sprinkle with the remaining basil, and serve.

Prep = 15 minutes   **Chill** = 30 minutes   **Cook** = 3 minutes
Yield = 4 servings

8

Sweet Treats
and Desserts

Classic Bananas Foster

A book on cooking and baking with liquors and spirits would not be complete without Bananas Foster. Although it is a classic, it is made in many different ways. I have chosen intense dark rum, brandy, and sweet banana liqueur to bring my Bananas Foster together. Serve over vanilla bean ice cream right out of the pan.

- 8 tablespoons (1 stick, or 112 g) unsalted butter
- ³/₄ cup (167 g) packed dark brown sugar
- 4 ripe but firm bananas, sliced
- ¹/₃ cup (80 ml) dark rum
- 2 tablespoons (30 ml) brandy
- 2 tablespoons (30 ml) banana liqueur
- 1 teaspoon ground cinnamon
- 1 teaspoon pure vanilla extract
- Vanilla ice cream, for serving

In a large skillet over high heat, melt the butter. Add the brown sugar and stir to dissolve. Add the bananas in an even layer, spooning the sauce over the top of the them, and cook for 2 minutes, turning once. Standing back from the heat, carefully add the dark rum, brandy, and banana liqueur, swirling the pan to combine the ingredients. Turn the bananas, sprinkle with cinnamon and add the vanilla, and turn the bananas again, spooning sauce over the top of them. Scoop ice cream into 4 individual serving bowls and top with the warm bananas and sauce.

Prep = 5 minutes **Cook** = 10 minutes **Yield** = 4 servings

Italian Spumoni with Amaretto

Peppered among the numerous and fantastic restaurants and shops in any Italian neighborhood are some of the finest pastry and gelato sellers around. Spumoni is one of the confections you will find there. Relatively simple to make with just a bit of mixing, the result is delicious.

6	large eggs, at room temperature
1/2	cup (100 g) granulated sugar
1/2	teaspoon grated nutmeg
1/2	cup (120 ml) Marsala wine
3	tablespoons (45 ml) amaretto liqueur
1 1/2	cups (350 ml) heavy cream
4	amaretto biscotti, crumbled

Fill a large mixing bowl with ice cubes and set aside. Bring water to a simmer in the base of a double boiler. Separate the eggs, placing the yolks in the top of the double boiler (off the heat) and the whites in a mixing bowl. Add the sugar and nutmeg to the egg yolks and beat with a handheld mixer until they are thickened and form a ribbon. Add the Marsala and amaretto, stirring to combine. Set the pan of yolk mixture in the base of the double boiler and beat over low heat until foamy and thickened, 3 to 5 minutes. Transfer the top pan to the ice bath, whisking until cooled. In the separate bowl, beat the egg whites until soft peaks form, then set aside. Beat the cream in a third bowl until soft peaks form. Fold all three mixtures together slowly, in the cream bowl, using a rubber spatula. Pour into an ice-cream maker and chill according to the manufacturer's directions. Transfer to an airtight container and freeze at least 4 hours, until hardened. Serve scoops topped with crumbled biscotti.

Prep = 30 minutes **Chill** =6 hours
Yield = 4 cups (550 g)

Añejo Truffles

The addition of espresso and coffee liqueur made with tequila simply make the classic chocolate truffle better. The rich taste of chocolate with the mellow depth of espresso is a delicious treat.

- 4 tablespoons ($\frac{1}{2}$ stick, or 55 g) unsalted butter
- 8 ounces (225 g) semisweet chocolate chips or squares, chopped
- $\frac{1}{4}$ cup (60 ml) heavy cream
- $\frac{1}{4}$ teaspoon pure vanilla extract
- $\frac{1}{4}$ cup (60 ml) coffee tequila, such as Patrón XO Café
- 1 tablespoon (7 g) instant espresso powder dissolved in 1 teaspoon hot water

  Unsweetened cocoa powder or confectioners' sugar, for dusting

In the top bowl of a double boiler, melt the butter and chocolate with the heavy cream. Add the vanilla, coffee tequila, and espresso mixture; stir to combine. Pour the chocolate into a container and refrigerate until cooled completely, at least 2 hours. Scoop out the chocolate, using either a tablespoon or a small (1-ounce [30 g]) ice-cream scoop. Gently roll the scoops into balls and dust with cocoa powder or confectioners' sugar.

Prep = 10 minutes **Chill** = 2 hours **Yield** = about 24 truffles

Coconut Rum Key Lime Cake

This coconut lime cake is a tropical delight. The moist, decadent cake is drizzled with a lime-rum sauce.

1	cup (70 g) sweetened flaked coconut
8	tablespoons (1 stick, 112 g) butter, softened
1	cup (200 g) granulated sugar
1/4	cup (55 g) firmly packed light brown sugar
1	tablespoon (7 g) grated Key lime or regular lime zest
2	large eggs
1	cup (110 g) all-purpose flour
3/4	cup (83 g) ground oatmeal
1 1/2	teaspoons baking powder
3/4	cup (175 ml) coconut milk
5	tablespoons (75 ml) fresh Key lime juice
4	teaspoons (20 ml) light rum
1	cup (100 g) confectioners' sugar

Preheat the oven to 350ºF (180ºC, or gas mark 4). Butter the sides and bottom of a 9-inch (23 cm) round cake pan with at least 2-inch (5 cm) sides. Line the bottom with parchment paper and butter that. Spread the coconut on a sheet pan and toast until lightly golden, 6 to 8 minutes. Watch closely, because it can burn quickly. In the bowl of a stand mixer fitted with the paddle attachment, beat the butter, sugars, and lime zest until smooth and creamy. Add the eggs, one at a time, beating well after each addition. In a bowl, stir together the flour, oatmeal, baking powder, and 1/2 cup (35 g) of the toasted coconut. In a separate bowl, stir together the coconut milk, 3 tablespoons (45 ml) lime juice, and 2 teaspoons (10 ml) of light rum. Gradually add half of the flour mixture to the sugar mixture, then slowly add the coconut milk mixture, ending with the remaining flour mixture. Scrape into the prepared pan, place on middle rack of the oven, and bake for 40 to 45 minutes, until a toothpick inserted comes out clean. Remove the cake from the oven and cool. Invert onto a plate; invert again onto a serving dish. Meanwhile, whisk together the confectioners' sugar and the remaining 2 tablespoons (30 ml) lime juice and 2 teaspoons (10 ml) of light rum. Pour the lime glaze over the cooled cake, sprinkle with the remaining 1/2 cup (35 g) toasted coconut, and serve.

Prep = 30 minutes **Bake** = 40 to 45 minutes **Cool** = about 1 hour
Yield = 10 servings

Polenta Puddings with Ouzo and Caramelized Peaches

Ouzo adds a delicate but flavorful touch to these individual puddings. Creamy polenta and the freshness of summer peaches create a beautiful dessert.

- ¼ cup (60 ml) ouzo or grappa
- ¼ cup (41 g) golden raisins
- 2 cups (475 ml) whole milk
- ⅛ teaspoon sea salt
- ¼ cup (60 ml) peach nectar
- ¾ cup (160 g) Italian polenta
- 1 cup (250 g) whole milk ricotta cheese
- ½ cup (100 g) granulated sugar
- ¼ teaspoon ground cinnamon
- ½ teaspoon pure vanilla extract
- 3 eggs, lightly beaten

PEACHES:
- 4 tablespoons (½ stick, or 55 g) unsalted butter
- 4 peaches, peeled, pitted and thickly sliced
- ⅓ cup (82 g) chopped pecans
- 3 whole cloves
- 1 tablespoon (14 g) packed light brown sugar
- 1 teaspoon ground cinnamon
- ¼ cup (60 ml) port
- 2 tablespoons (40 g) honey
- 1 tablespoon (15 ml) ouzo or grappa

In a saucepan over medium heat, warm the ouzo. Remove from the heat and add the raisins. Let stand for 30 minutes. In a large saucepan over high heat, stir together the milk, peach nectar, and salt. Bring to a boil, slowly whisk in the polenta, lower the heat to medium, and cook, whisking, for 2 to 3 minutes. Continue to cook the polenta, stirring only occasionally, until thickened, about 15 minutes. Preheat oven to 375°F (190°C, or gas mark 5). Butter six ½-cup (120 ml) ramekins. In a large bowl, stir together the ricotta cheese, sugar, cinnamon, and vanilla. Add the polenta, stirring well. Drain the raisins, reserving 2 tablespoons (30 ml) of the soaking brandy, and add them to the polenta. Add the eggs, stirring to combine. Divide the mixture evenly among the ramekins. Place the ramekins on a sheet pan and place on the middle rack of the oven. Bake until a skewer inserted into the center of one pudding comes out clean, about 25 minutes. Remove from the oven and let rest for 5 minutes on a cooling rack.

For the peaches: In a large skillet, melt the butter over medium heat. Add the peaches and pecans, stir lightly and gently to coat with the butter. Add the cloves, brown sugar, and cinnamon and cook for 3 minutes. Add the port and cook for 1 minute. Add the honey, ouzo, and reserved 2 tablespoons (30 ml) of ouzo from soaking the raisins, stirring to combine. Cook for an additional 5 minutes, until the peaches are tender and browned. Invert the ramekins to release the puddings onto individual dessert plates. Spoon the caramelized peaches over the top of each pudding. Serve warm.

Prep = 30 minutes **Cook** = 55 minutes **Yield** = 6 servings

Pumpkin-Spiced Croissant Bread Pudding

There isn't any other word for this one but *wow!*
Enjoy this with Spiced Rum Whipped Cream.

8	cups (400 g) torn day-old butter croissants
1	cup (150 g) mini marshmallows
4	eggs
1/4	cup (50 g) granulated sugar
1 1/2	cups (350 ml) milk
1/2	cup (120 ml) heavy cream
1/2	cup (120 ml) spiced rum
1	teaspoon pure vanilla extract
1 1/2	teaspoons pumpkin pie spice
1	cup (225 g) pumpkin puree

Preheat the oven to 350ºF (180°C, or gas mark 4). Spray a 9 × 12-inch (23 × 30.5 cm) baking dish with nonstick cooking spray. Place the torn croissants in the baking dish, spreading evenly. Sprinkle the marshmallows over the croissant pieces, working them down and into the croissants evenly. Leave several of the marshmallows exposed on the top. In a large mixing bowl, whip the eggs until smooth. To the eggs add the sugar, milk, heavy cream, rum, vanilla, pumpkin pie spice, and pumpkin purée, whisking together briskly until well combined. Pour the mixture slowly over the croissants, spreading it evenly and allowing it to soak in. Gently press the top croissants into the liquid just to lightly cover. Bake on the middle rack of the oven for 35 minutes, until golden brown and the marshmallows on top are melted. Remove from the oven, let cool for 5 minutes on a cooling rack, then serve warm with the Spiced Rum Whipped Cream.

FOR THE SPICED RUM WHIPPED CREAM:

1 cup (240 ml) whipping cream
3 tablespoons (38 g) granulated sugar
1 teaspoon spiced rum

In the bowl of a mixer fitted with the whip attachment combine the cream, sugar, and spiced rum. Whip on high until stiff peaks form, about 7 minutes. Refrigerate until ready to use.

Prep = 15 minutes **Bake** = 35 minutes **Yield** = 6 to 8 servings

Chocolate Coffee Pots de Crème with Spiced Pecans

A classic French dessert, pots de crème are simply that: little pots of velvety, rich cream or custard. These, a marriage of chocolate and espresso, hide a chili powder punch. The chili pepper pecans add a delightful salty crunch. Pots de crème are an effortless dessert with an elegant result.

6	ounces (170 g) fine-quality bittersweet chocolate, finely chopped
1 ½	cups (350 ml) heavy cream
⅓	cup (80 ml) whole milk
1 ½	tablespoons (12 g) instant espresso powder
½	teaspoon ancho chili powder
6	large egg yolks
3	tablespoons (38 g) granulated sugar
¼	teaspoon ground nutmeg
¼	cup (60 ml) coffee liqueur, such as Kahlúa
1 ½	teaspoons pure vanilla extract

CANDIED PECANS:

⅓	cup (83 g) roughly chopped pecans
1	tablespoon (14 g) butter
1	tablespoon (14 g) firmly packed brown sugar
¼	teaspoon ground nutmeg
¼	teaspoon ancho chili powder
¼	teaspoon ground cinnamon
	Pinch of salt and black pepper
½	teaspoon granulated sugar

Preheat the oven to 300°F (150°C, or gas mark 2) and position a rack in the center. Prepare a deep-sided roasting pan by layering a double thickness of paper towels on the bottom. Place six ½-cup (120 ml) custard cups, ramekins, or pot de crème cups in the pan. Bring 4 cups (950 ml) of water to a boil and set aside.

Place the chocolate in a heatproof bowl. In a large saucepan over medium-high heat, heat the cream with the milk just until boiling, add the espresso powder, and ancho chili powder, and stir to dissolve. Pour half of the cream mixture over the chocolate, stirring with a wooden spoon or rubber spatula until the chocolate is melted and smooth. In a mixing bowl, whisk the egg yolks with the sugar and nutmeg until creamy and smooth. Gradually, in a slow, steady stream, whisking all the while, pour the remaining warmed milk mixture over the egg mixture to combine. Add the hot liquid slowly because this will temper the eggs without scrambling them as they thicken the mixture. Stir in the coffee liqueur and vanilla. Slowly pour the egg mixture into the melted chocolate, stirring gently to combine. Using a spoon, skim any foam from the top of the custard.

Divide the custard evenly among the cups. Pour enough of the hot water into the pan to rise halfway up the sides of the cups. Cover the pan tightly with aluminum foil, piercing a few holes around the top of the foil. If using pot de crème cups with their own lids, those lids are enough for a cover. Carefully place the pan in the oven. Bake until the custards are set around edges but still have movement to them, 30 to 40 minutes. Gently remove from the oven and let rest in the pan on a cooling rack, covered, for 10 minutes. Uncover and transfer the ramekins to a cooling rack for 1 hour. Pots de crème may be served at room temperature, or if you prefer cover with plastic wrap and chill until cold throughout, at least 3 hours.

For the candied pecans: Melt the butter in a medium skillet over medium heat. Add the pecans, brown sugar, nutmeg, chili powder, cinnamon, and salt and black pepper. Stir the pecans with the spices until well coated and toasted, being careful not to burn. Transfer the pecans to a sheet of aluminum foil or parchment paper, sprinkle with the granulated sugar, and allow to cool. When ready to serve, crumble the pecans over the top of each custard.

Prep = 30 minutes **Bake** = 40 minutes **Cool** = 1 to 3 hours
Yield = 6 servings

Irish Cream Fudge

Fudge with a rich, creamy caramel taste of Irish cream—is there a better sweet treat? For variations, use mint- or caramel-flavored Irish cream, or reduce Irish cream to ½ cup (120 ml) and add ¼ cup (60 ml) coffee liqueur.

1 ½	cups (180 g) finely chopped walnuts
6	cups (1.2 kg) granulated sugar
1 ½	cups (355 ml) evaporated milk
½	cup (170 g) light corn syrup
8	tablespoons (1 stick or 112g) unsalted butter
3	tablespoons (60 g) honey
½	teaspoon salt
¾	cup (175 ml) Irish cream liqueur
2 ¼	cups (395 g) semisweet chocolate chips, melted

Spread the walnuts evenly on the bottom of a lightly greased 8 × 11-inch (20.3 × 28 cm) baking dish with 2-inch (5 cm) -high sides.

Spray the sides of a large stockpot lightly with nonstick cooking spray. In the stockpot, combine the sugar, evaporated milk, corn syrup, butter, honey, and salt. Place over medium-low heat and cook, stirring constantly, until the sugar dissolves. Using a pastry brush dipped in warm water, brush down the sides of the pot while cooking to prevent sugar crystals from forming.

Submerge a candy thermometer into the pan, making sure it is not touching the bottom. Increase the heat to medium-high and without stirring, bring to a boil. Cook the mixture until the syrup reaches the soft-ball stage, 234° to 240°F (112° to 115°C). Fill the kitchen sink to a 2-inch (5 cm) depth with cold water. Transfer the stockpot to the sink, submerging in the water. Add the Irish cream to the mixture, but do not stir. Allow the syrup to cool to 110°F (43°C) and add the chocolate. Using an electric hand mixer, beat the fudge on medium speed until it is dull and thickens. Pour the fudge evenly over the walnuts, spreading in an even layer in the pan, and set aside to cool completely. Cut into 1-inch (2.5 cm) squares and serve, or store in an airtight container in the refrigerator for up to 2 weeks.

Prep = 10 minutes **Cook** = 30 minutes **Cool** = 30 minutes
Yield = about 7 dozen squares

Bananas Foster Cake

Bananas Foster is too good to only have one way. This version is more portable. Take this one on the road when you are responsible for the dessert. I promise it will surprise and please.

2 ½	cups (275 g) all-purpose flour
2	teaspoons baking powder
½	teaspoon salt
1	teaspoon ground cinnamon
½	cup (120 ml) milk
½	cup (120 ml) coconut milk
1	tablespoon (15 ml) dark rum
1	tablespoon (15 ml) banana liqueur
16	tablespoons (2 sticks, or 225 g) unsalted butter, softened
1	cup (200 g) granulated sugar
½	cup (112 g) packed dark brown sugar
3	eggs
1	egg yolk
1	cup (225 g) mashed bananas

Preheat the oven to 375°F (190°C, or gas mark 5). Coat the bottom and sides of a 9-inch (22.9 cm) springform pan with nonstick cooking spray or butter. In a bowl, whisk together the flour, baking powder, salt, and cinnamon, then set aside. In another bowl, whisk together the milk, coconut milk, rum, and banana liqueur, and set aside. In the bowl of a stand mixer fitted with the blade attachment, combine the butter and sugars and beat on high until creamy and smooth, about 5 minutes. Scrape the beater and sides of the bowl and beat again for 1 minute. Add the eggs and yolk one at a time, beating on high after each addition until well combined. Scrape the beater and sides of the bowl again. Alternating between the two, add the flour mixture and milk mixture in 1-cup (110 g) increments, beginning and ending with the flour mixture, beating well after each addition. Add the bananas and blend to combine. Pour the mixture into the prepared pan and bake for 45 minutes, until golden and a toothpick inserted into the center comes out clean. Transfer to a cooling rack and let cool for 15 minutes. Remove the sides of the pan and place the cake on a serving platter.

Prep = 20 minutes **Bake** = 45 Minutes **Cool** = 15 minutes
Yield = 12 servings

Citrus Cheesecake with Shortbread Crust

Light, moist, tart, and tangy, this cheesecake is a winner, blanketed in a shortbread-almond crust. The filling is a triple-threat combination of Limoncello, orange, and lime. The result is a burst of citrus flavor with a subtle layer of almond for balance.

CRUST:

- 8 ounces (225 g) shortbread cookies
- 2 ounces (55 g) Marcona almonds
- 1 tablespoon (13 g) granulated sugar
- 2 tablespoons (28 g) butter, melted

FILLING:

- 3 (8-ounce [225 g]) packages cream cheese, softened
- 1 cup (225 g) sour cream, at room temperature
- 1 cup (200 g) granulated sugar
- 4 eggs
- ¼ cup (60 ml) lime juice
- 2 tablespoons (30 ml) Limoncello liqueur
- 1 teaspoon almond extract
- Grated zest of 1 orange

LIMONCELLO CURD:

- ½ cup (100 g) granulated sugar
- 1½ teaspoons cornstarch
- ¼ cup plus 2 tablespoons (90 ml) freshly squeezed lemon juice
- ¼ cup (60 ml) Limoncello liqueur
- 3 tablespoons (45 ml) heavy cream
- 3 eggs
- 2 egg yolks

½ cup (62 g) chopped toasted Marcona almonds, for garnish

For the crust: Place the shortbread cookies and almonds in the bowl of a food processor fitted with the blade attachment and pulse until finely ground. Transfer to a bowl, add the sugar and butter, and stir until evenly moistened. Press the mixture onto the bottom and 2 inches (5 cm) up the sides of a 9-inch (23 cm) round springform pan. Cover with plastic wrap and refrigerate until ready to use. Preheat the oven to 300°F (150°C, or gas mark 2).

For the filling: In the bowl of a mixer fitted with the paddle attachment, beat the cream cheese until smooth, about 3 minutes. Using a rubber spatula, scrape the bowl and paddle. Add the sour cream and beat until smooth. Add the sugar ½ cup (100 g) at a time, beating until well incorporated and smooth, about 2 minutes. Add the eggs one at a time, beating well after each addition. Scrape the bowl and paddle again and add the lime juice, Limoncello, almond extract, and orange zest. Beat for 2 additional minutes to incorporate. Pour the batter over the prepared crust, and place the pan on a sheet pan to catch any drips. Bake on the middle rack of the oven for about 2 hours, until a toothpick inserted into the center comes out clean. Transfer the cake to a cooling rack and let cool for 20 minutes. Cover loosely and refrigerate for at least 2 hours or overnight before serving.

For the curd: In a small saucepan, stir together the sugar and cornstarch. Stir in the lemon juice and Limoncello until well incorporated. Place the pan over medium heat, add the cream, and whisk until combined. Add the eggs and yolks one at a time, whisking after each addition until well combined. Once the sauce is thickened, remove from the heat, pour into a container, and let cool for 10 minutes. Cover with plastic wrap laid directly on the curd, and refrigerate for at least 1 hour or overnight.

To serve, remove the sides from the springform pan and place the cake on a serving plate. Spread the Limoncello curd evenly over the top of the cake. Sprinkle with the toasted almonds, slice, and serve.

Prep = 50 minutes **Bake** = 2 hours **Chill** = at least 2 hours
Yield = 12 servings

Coconut Key Lime Cake

It's hard for me to say because I love sweets, but Key lime pie is probably my most favorite dessert.

- 1 ¾ cups (193 g) all-purpose flour
- 1 ½ teaspoons baking powder
- ½ teaspoon salt
- 8 tablespoons (1 stick, or 112 g) unsalted butter, softened
- ¾ cup (150 g) granulated sugar
- 3 eggs, at room temperature
- 1 ½ teaspoons coconut extract
- ½ teaspoon rum extract
- ½ cup (120 ml) coconut milk
- 1 cup (70 g) sweetened shredded coconut, toasted
- 2 tablespoons (30 ml) Key lime juice

MANGO TOPPING:

- 2 large, ripe mangoes, seeded and cubed
- 2 teaspoons (30 ml) Key lime juice
- 2 teaspoons granulated sugar
- ½ cup (120 ml) coconut rum

Preheat the oven to 325°F (170°C, or gas mark 3). Butter and flour a 9 × 5 × 4-inch (23 × 12.5 × 10 cm) loaf pan. In a bowl, whisk together the flour, baking powder, and salt, then set aside. In the bowl of a mixer fitted with the paddle attachment, beat the butter and sugar until smooth and creamy, about 5 minutes. Add the eggs one at a time, beating well after each addition. Add the coconut and rum extracts and beat well. Add half the coconut milk and beat on low to combine. Scrape the sides of the bowl and the beater, add the remaining coconut milk, and beat to combine. Add the coconut and lime juice and beat on low just to combine. Scrape the batter into the prepared pan and bake for 1 hour, until a toothpick inserted into the center comes out clean. Transfer to a cooling rack and let cool for 15 minutes, turn the cake out of the pan, and allow to cool completely.

For the mango topping: In a saucepan over medium heat, combine the mangoes, lime juice, sugar, and rum and bring to a boil, stirring until the sugar is dissolved. Remove from the heat and set aside to cool. Slice the cooled cake and serve with the mango topping.

Prep = 20 minutes   **Bake** = 1 hour
Yield = 10 servings

Frangelico Brownies

If you frequent bakeries, there are usually piles of decadent chocolate brownies. This brownie is no-fuss, no-muss with not a lot of extras, just a pure celebration of chocolate and one of its finest complements, hazelnuts—simple, traditional, fudgey, and cakey.

6	ounces (170 g) dark chocolate, chopped
8	tablespoons (1 stick, or 112 g) unsalted butter, softened
1 1/4	cups (250 g) granulated sugar
	Pinch of salt
2	eggs, at room temperature
1/4	cup (60 ml) hazelnut liqueur, such as Frangelico
1/2	teaspoon pure vanilla extract
3/4	cup (83 g) all-purpose flour
1/2	cup (63 g) unsweetened cocoa powder
1/2	cup (63 g) toasted, chopped hazelnuts

Preheat the oven to 325°F (170°C, or gas mark 3). Grease an 8-inch (20.5 cm) square baking pan with nonstick cooking spray. Line with two sheets of parchment paper that over hang the sides of the pan, acting as handles with which to remove the brownies. Melt the chocolate in the top of a double boiler and set aside. In the bowl of stand mixer fitted with the blade attachment, beat the butter and sugar until smooth, then add the salt, eggs, hazelnut liqueur, and vanilla and beat to just combine. Beat in the melted chocolate. Add the flour and cocoa powder, beating to just incorporate. Mix in the nuts by hand. Pour the batter into the prepared pan and bake on the middle rack of the oven for 40 to 50 minutes, until firm and the sides begin to pull away from the sides of the pan. Remove from the oven and let cool completely in the pan on a cooling rack. Remove from the pan and cut into 16 squares.

Prep = 20 minutes **Bake** = 40 to 50 minutes **Yield** = 16 brownies

Italian Ice or Granita, Five Ways

Orange Campari

3	cups (710 ml)	strained freshly squeezed orange juice
1	cup (235 ml)	Campari
1 ½	cups (300 g)	granulated sugar
		Zest and juice of 1 lemon

In a nonreactive saucepan over medium heat, combine the orange juice, Campari, and sugar. Bring to a boil, stirring until the sugar is dissolved, 5 minutes. Remove from the heat and stir in the lemon zest and juice. Pour the mixture into a large, shallow metal baking pan and freeze until icy, about 4 hours. Using a fork, break up the ice and freeze for an additional 2 hours. Break up again, and refreeze for at least one hour. Serve broken up or scooped into bowls.

Italian Lemon Ice

2	cups (475 ml)	strained freshly squeezed lemon juice
½	cup (120 ml)	water
1	cup (235 ml)	Limoncello liqueur
2	cups (400 g)	granulated sugar
		Zest of 1 lemon

In a nonreactive saucepan over medium heat, combine the lemon juice, water, Limoncello, and sugar. Bring to a boil, stirring until the sugar is dissolved, 5 minutes. Remove from the heat and stir in the lemon zest. Pour the mixture into a large, shallow metal baking pan and freeze until icy, about 4 hours. Using a fork, break up the ice and freeze for an additional 2 hours. Break up again, and refreeze for at least one hour. Serve broken up or scooped into bowls.

Prep = 10 minutes **Freeze** = 6 hours **Yield** = 6 servings

Raspberry Chambord Ice

  2 cups (475 ml) water
 ½ cup (120 ml) strained freshly squeezed orange juice
  1 cup (235 ml) Chambord liqueur
  2 cups (400 g) granulated sugar
  2 cups (220 g) fresh or frozen raspberries
    Zest of 1 orange

In a nonreactive saucepan over medium heat, combine the water, orange juice, Chambord, and sugar. Bring to a boil, stirring until the sugar is dissolved, 5 minutes. Add the berries and cook, stirring, for 5 minutes. Remove from the heat and stir in the orange zest. Using a stick blender, purée until the mixture is smooth. Pour the mixture into a large, shallow metal baking pan and freeze until icy, about 4 hours. Using a fork, break up the ice and freeze for an additional 2 hours. Break up again, and refreeze for at least one hour. Serve broken up or scooped into bowls.

Prep = 15 minutes **Freeze** = 6 hours **Yield** = 8 servings

Melons and Midori

Midori is a melon liqueur that brightens the flavor of any garden-fresh, ripened melon.

- 6 cups (1 k) assorted, seeded, cubed firm melons, such as canary, musk, honeydew, or cantaloupe
- 2 cups (300 g) halved green grapes
- 1 cup (120 ml) Midori
- 2 tablespoons (25 g) granulated sugar
- ¼ cup (60 ml) fresh orange juice
- 1 tablespoon (15 ml) lemon juice
- ¼ cup (15 g) torn mint leaves

Combine the melon and grapes in a large, transparent trifle dish and toss gently to combine. In a bowl, whisk together the Midori, sugar, and orange and lemon juices. Pour over the fruit, cover with plastic wrap, and refrigerate for at least 1 hour, stirring every 15 minutes to coat with juices. Just before serving, remove from the refrigerator and toss the fruit with the mint.

Prep = 15 minutes **Chill** = 1 hour **Yield** = 8 servings

Tipsy Watermelon and Blueberries

Every time I serve this summer favorite, I first hear, "We couldn't possibly eat all that watermelon," and then I hear, "Is there any more?" This simple and delicious summer treat is perfect when the fruits are at their ripest.

1 medium chilled, seedless watermelon, rind and seeds removed, cut into wedges

2 cups (290 g) fresh blueberries

4 cups (950 ml) coconut rum

1 cup (235 ml) citrus-flavored vodka

$1/4$ cup (60 ml) pineapple juice

$1/4$ cup (15 g) chopped coarsely packed mint leaves

In a large glass jar with a lid (such as an apothecary jar), layer the watermelon slices with the blueberries, stacking the fruit to the top of the jar. In a large pot or bowl, stir together the rum, vodka, pineapple juice, and mint. Pour the mixture over the fruit in the jar. Cover and refrigerate for at least 30 minutes before serving. Use the liquid from the jar to make cocktails, if you like.

Prep = 20 minutes **Chill** = 30 minutes **Yield** = 10 servings

Kahlúa Chocolate Chip Cookies

Chocolate chip cookies go mocha, in this twist on an old favorite.

16	tablespoons (2 sticks, or 225 g) unsalted butter, softened
1	cup (200 g) granulated sugar
½	cup (112 g) packed light brown sugar
3	eggs, at room temperature
2 ½	cups (275 g) all-purpose flour
1	teaspoon baking soda
1 ½	teaspoons baking powder
½	teaspoon salt
1	tablespoon (7 g) espresso powder
1	teaspoon pure vanilla extract
¼	cup (60 ml) coffee liqueur, such as Kahlúa
1 ½	cups (260 g) semisweet chocolate chips
¾	cup (93 g) chopped pecans

Preheat the oven to 350ºF (180°C, or gas mark 4). In the bowl of a stand mixer fitted with the paddle attachment, beat the butter and sugars until smooth and creamy, about 7 minutes. Add the eggs one at a time, mixing well after each addition. In a separate bowl, whisk together the flour, baking soda, baking powder, and salt. In a small bowl, mix the espresso powder and vanilla with the coffee liqueur, stirring until the espresso powder is dissolved. Add the flour mixture ½ cup (55 g) at a time to the butter mixture, blending well after each addition and scraping the sides of the bowl as needed. Add the coffee liqueur mixture and blend to combine. Remove the bowl from the mixer, scraping the paddle and sides of the bowl. Add the chocolate chips and pecans, stirring to combine. Using a 2-ounce (55 g) ice-cream scoop, place mounds of cookie dough on ungreased baking sheets. Bake on the center rack of the oven for 10 to 12 minutes, until just turning golden on top. Remove from the oven and let cool for 2 minutes on the baking sheets, then transfer to a cooling rack to cool completely. Store in an airtight container for up to 3 days.

Prep = 20 minutes **Bake** = 10 to 12 minutes
Yield = 3 dozen cookies

Browned Butter Amaretto Cookies

Browning butter is a technique that adds a unique, robust flavor to both sweet and savory dishes. The technique simply toasts the milk solids in butter until golden with a nutty aroma.

16	tablespoons (2 sticks, or 225 g) unsalted butter
3	cups (330 g) all-purpose flour
2	teaspoons (9.2 g) baking powder
1/4	teaspoon ground cardamom
1 3/4	cups (350 g) granulated sugar
3	eggs, at room temperature
1/4	cup (60 ml) amaretto liqueur
1	teaspoon grated orange zest
2/3	cup (88 g) pine nuts

In a small saucepan, melt the butter over medium-high heat. Once the butter begins to boil, lower the heat to medium. Stirring occasionally, let the butter cook until the foam subsides and it begins to have toasted brown bits. The butter will take on an amber color and a nutty aroma. As soon as the aroma turns nutty, remove from the heat and set aside to cool completely. In a large bowl, whisk together the flour, baking powder, and cardamom and set aside.

Preheat the oven to 350ºF (180ºC, or gas mark 4). Spray baking sheets with nonstick cooking spray. In the bowl of a stand mixer fitted with the paddle attachment, beat together the cooled browned butter and the sugar until smooth and fluffy, about 4 minutes. Add the eggs one at a time, beating well after each addition. Add the amaretto and orange zest and beat to combine. Add the dry ingredients 1 cup (110 g) at a time, blending after each addition and scraping the sides of the bowl and the paddle, beating to just combine. Remove the bowl from the mixer and clean the paddle.

Prep = 20 minutes **Bake** = 12 to 14 minutes
Yield = 4 dozen cookies

Stir in the ⅓ cup (44 g) of pine nuts to just combine. Using a 1-ounce (30 g) ice-cream scoop, place mounds of the dough on the prepared baking sheets with about 2 inches (5 cm) between them. Press a few of the reserved pine nuts into the tops to form a starburst (about six pine nuts per cookie). Bake on the middle rack of the oven for 12 to 14 minutes, just until the edges and tops begin to turn golden brown. Let cool on the baking sheets for 2 minutes, then transfer to a cooling rack to cool completely. Store in an airtight container for up to 3 days.

Figs with Mascarpone and Sambuca Honey

I grew up with a fig tree in my grandmother's backyard. Plucking those ripe, delicate, flavorful fruit from the branches and popping them into my mouth was a childhood dream. I could never wait to get inside to share them. Now I love figs as an elegant dessert.

- ¼ cup (80 g) good-quality honey
- 2 tablespoons (30 ml) sambuca
- 8 mint leaves, thinly sliced
- ½ pound (225 g) ripe Black Mission figs, quartered
- ½ cup (60 g) mascarpone cheese
- 1 brioche, sliced and toasted

In a small saucepan over low heat, warm the honey with the sambuca, stirring constantly, just until steam rises from the pan. Remove from the heat and let cool for 30 minutes; once cool, stir in the mint. Divide the figs, mascarpone, and slices of brioche among 4 dessert plates. Drizzle each with the sambuca honey and serve.

Prep = 10 minutes **Cool** = 30 minutes **Yield** = 4 servings

Holiday Rum-Soaked Cake

Tortuga, Haiti, is famous for its rich, heavenly rum cakes. Many of the rum cake recipes use boxed cake mixes, but this one goes all the way to the basics.

2 ½ cups (275 g) cake flour
½ teaspoon baking powder
¼ teaspoon ground nutmeg
½ teaspoon salt
16 tablespoons (2 sticks, or 225 g) unsalted butter, softened
1 cup (200 g) granulated sugar
⅓ cup (75 g) packed light brown sugar
5 eggs
½ teaspoon pure vanilla extract
½ teaspoon rum extract
1 tablespoon (15 ml) dark rum
½ cup chopped walnuts

TOPPING:
¼ cup (60 ml) water
¼ cup (60 ml) dark rum
1 cup (200 g) granulated sugar
4 tablespoons (1 stick, or 55 g) unsalted butter

Preheat the oven to 350ºF (180ºC, or gas mark 4). Butter and flour a 9 × 5 × 4-inch (23 × 12.5 × 10 cm) loaf pan. In a bowl, whisk flour, baking powder, nutmeg, and salt; set aside. In the bowl of a stand mixer fitted with the paddle attachment, beat the butter and the sugars until creamy, about 7 minutes. Add the eggs one at a time, beating well after each and scraping the sides of the bowl and the paddle. Add the vanilla, rum extract, and dark rum, and beat to combine. Add the flour mixture; beat to just incorporate, and stir in the walnuts. Scrape the batter into the prepared loaf pan. Bake for 65 minutes, until golden and a toothpick inserted into the center comes out clean. Transfer the pan to a cooling rack for 20 minutes.

For the topping: In a saucepan, combine the water, rum, sugar, and butter and cook, stirring, until the sugar is dissolved and the butter is melted. Boil for 1 minute. Leaving the cake in the pan, puncture the top at ½ (1.3 cm) inch intervals with a skewer, and slowly pour the topping over the cake, allowing it to soak in. Allow the cake to sit for 30 minutes before inverting it onto a serving plate.

Prep = 20 minutes **Bake** = 65 minutes **Cool** = 30 minutes
Yield = 8 servings

Spiced St-Germain Cake

St-Germain is a unique liqueur flavored with elder-flowers. Use spiced rum if you are unable to find it.

- 2 cups (220 g) cake flour
- 1 cup (110 g) ground oats
- 1 1/2 teaspoons baking powder
- 1 teaspoon baking soda
- 1 teaspoon ground cardamom
- 1/4 teaspoon salt
- 1/4 teaspoon ground ginger
- 1/4 teaspoon ground cinnamon
- 16 tablespoons (2 sticks, or 225 g) unsalted butter
- 1 1/2 cups (300 g) granulated sugar
- 1/4 cup (55 g) packed light brown sugar
- 5 eggs
- 1 1/2 cups (190 g) finely ground walnuts
- 1 teaspoon vanilla extract
- 3/4 cup (180 ml) St-Germain
- 1 cup (235 ml) sour cream
- Confectioners' sugar, for dusting

Preheat the oven to 325°F (170°C, or gas mark 3). Grease and flour a 10-inch (25.5 cm) tube cake pan. In a bowl, whisk together the flour, oats, baking powder, baking soda, cardamom, salt, ginger, and cinnamon; set aside. In the bowl of a stand mixer fitted with the paddle attachment, beat the butter and the sugars until creamy, about 8 minutes. Add the eggs one at a time, beating well after each, scraping the sides of the bowl and the paddle. Add 1 cup (125 g) of walnuts, vanilla, and 1/4 cup (60 ml) of the St-Germain liqueur and blend for 3 minutes. Add the flour mixture, alternating with sour cream, beginning and ending with the flour mixture, blending well. Scrape the batter into the prepared pan and bake for 45 to 50 minutes, until the cake begins to pull away from the sides of the pan. Transfer the cake pan to a cooling rack for 15 minutes. Meanwhile, place the remaining 1/2 cup (120 ml) St-Germain liqueur and the remaining 1/2 cup (65 g) of walnuts in a saucepan over medium heat. Let it reduce by half. Turn the cake out of the pan and set it upright on the cooling rack. Set the cooling rack with the cake on a sheet pan to catch the drips. Spoon the St-Germain sauce over the cake, letting it soak in. Sprinkle lightly with the confectioners' sugar, slice, and serve.

Prep = 20 minutes **Bake** = 45 to 50 minutes **Yield** = 12 servings

Strawberries with Balsamic and Sambuca

Wine-based balsamic vinegar and anise-flavored sambuca are a winning combination with fresh strawberries.

- ½ cup (120 ml) balsamic vinegar
- 2 tablespoons (25 g) granulated sugar
- ¼ cup (60 ml) sambuca liqueur
- 1 tablespoon (20 g) honey
- 1 teaspoon culinary lavender (optional)
- 1 cup (235 ml) heavy cream
- ½ teaspoon pure vanilla extract
- 6 slices pound cake
- 1 pint (350 g) fresh strawberries, hulled and halved

In a saucepan over medium heat, combine the balsamic vinegar, 1 tablespoon (13 g) of the sugar, the sambuca, and honey. Bring to a boil, then decrease the heat to low. Cook until the sugar is dissolved and the sauce has thickened enough that it coats the back of a spoon. Remove from the heat and stir in the lavender Whip the heavy cream on high with the remaining 1 tablespoon (12 g) of sugar and the vanilla until stiff peaks form, about 5 minutes. Place a slice of pound cake on each of 6 dessert plates, top with a sixth of the strawberries, drizzle the berries with the balsamic reduction, top with a dollop of whipped cream, and serve.

Prep = 15 minutes   **Yield** = 6 servings

Mixed Berry Pie with Oat and Almond Streusel

Pick the freshest berries at the peak of ripeness when they are packed with flavor. If the time of year doesn't allow for fresh berries, use frozen: Simply defrost slightly and drain a bit of the juices before mixing for the filling, reserving the strained juices to drizzle over the pie or ice cream.

CRUST:

- 1 1/2 cups (165 g) all-purpose flour
- 2 teaspoons granulated sugar
- 1/2 teaspoon salt
- 8 tablespoons (1 stick, or 112 g) cold unsalted butter, cut into small pieces
- 2 tablespoons (30 ml) ice water

TOPPING:

- 3/4 cup (83 g) all-purpose flour
- 1/2 cup (100 g) granulated sugar
- 2 tablespoons (16 g) finely chopped crystallized ginger
- 1 teaspoon finely grated orange zest
- 1/4 teaspoon salt
- 8 tablespoons (1 stick, or 112 g) cold unsalted butter, cut into small pieces
- 1 tablespoon (15 ml) orange juice
- 1 cup (92 g) sliced almonds
- 1/2 cup (38 g) rolled oats

FILLING:

- 2 cups (290 g) fresh blueberries
- 1 cup (110 g) fresh strawberries, hulled and sliced
- 2 cups (220 g) fresh raspberries
- 1 cup (110 g) fresh blackberries
- 1/2 cup (100 g) granulated sugar
- 1 tablespoon (15 ml) freshly squeezed lemon juice
- 2 tablespoons (30 ml) blackberry brandy
- 1/4 cup (32 g) cornstarch

For the crust: In the bowl of a food processor fitted with the blade attachment, combine the flour, sugar, and salt and pulse to combine. Add the butter and process until a coarse cornmeal consistency is reached. Add the water and pulse until the dough comes together in a ball. Add more water, 1 tablespoon (15 ml) at a time, if the mixture is too dry. Transfer the dough to a flat work surface and press out into a small disk. Wrap in plastic wrap or place in a resealable plastic bag and refrigerate for at least 1 hour. The dough can be made up to 2 days in advance. Let the dough come to room temperature before rolling out.

For the topping: In the bowl of the food processor, blend together the flour, sugar, ginger, orange zest, and salt. Add the butter and pulse until a crumbly texture is formed. Add the orange juice and pulse to just moisten. Transfer the mixture to a bowl and stir in the almonds and oats. Cover and chill. The topping can be made up to 1 day in advance.

Roll out the dough into a 12-inch (30.5 cm) round. Transfer to a 9-inch (23 cm) glass pie plate. Turn the edge of dough under, crimping into a decorative scalloped edge. Freeze until ready to use.

For the filling: Preheat the oven to 400°F (200°C, or gas mark 6) and place the rack in center of the oven. Gently toss together the blueberries, strawberries, raspberries, and blackberries with the sugar, lemon juice, brandy, and cornstarch; let stand for 10 minutes. Remove the dough from the freezer and pour in the berry mixture, mounding in the center. Place the pie on a sheet pan to catch any possible drips and bake for 30 minutes. Lower the oven temperature to 375°F (190°C, or gas mark 5). Sprinkle the topping evenly over the pie. Return the pie to the oven and bake for 30 to 40 minutes, until the crust and topping are golden brown. Transfer the pie to a cooling rack to cool completely.

Prep = 1 hour 30 minutes   **Bake** = 60 to 70 minutes
Yield = 8 to 10 servings

Chocolate Amaretto Mousse with Toasted Hazelnuts

Chocolate mousse is an elegant dish that isn't difficult to prepare, but it has an intense flavor that seems to have taken hours to achieve. This mousse has the tremendous flavor of chocolate, orange, and almond with the crunch of toasted hazelnuts on top.

10	ounces (280 g) dark chocolate, chopped
1/4	cup (60 ml) amaretto liqueur
2	tablespoons (30 ml) freshly squeezed orange juice
1 1/2	cups (350 ml) heavy cream
2	tablespoons (25 g) granulated sugar
1	teaspoon pure vanilla extract
1/4	cup (41 g) chopped hazelnuts

In a bowl over a pot of boiling water, melt the chocolate with the amaretto and orange juice, then set aside. In the bowl of a stand mixer fitted with the whip attachment, beat the heavy cream, sugar, and vanilla on high until stiff peaks form, about 5 minutes. Using a rubber spatula, gently fold half of the whipped cream mixture into the chocolate. Add the remaining whipped cream, folding until there are no more white streaks. Divide the mousse among 6 individual dishes, cover each with plastic wrap, and refrigerate for at least 2 hours and up to overnight. Toast the hazelnuts in a dry skillet or toaster oven until golden, sprinkle over each mousse, and serve.

Prep = 15 minutes **Cook** = at least 2 hours **Yield** = 6 servings

Bourbon-Poached Nectarines and Blackberry Parfaits

Sweet summer nectarines pair perfectly with the robust flavor of bourbon. As a poaching liquid, bourbon is lightly infused into the nectarines, imparting a subtle yet rich flavor. Use your favorite vanilla ice cream as the base for this fantastic treat.

4	cups (200 g) ½-inch (1.3 cm) cubes pound cake
5	tablespoons (70 g) unsalted butter
6	firm, ripe nectarines, sliced into wedges
½	cup (112 g) firmly packed light brown sugar
⅓	cup (80 ml) bourbon
2	tablespoons (28 ml) vanilla-flavored vodka
1	tablespoon (8 g) minced crystallized ginger
1	tablespoon (15 ml) white balsamic vinegar
1	pint (300 g) fresh blackberries
1	quart (570 g) good-quality vanilla ice cream
½	cup (40 g) vanilla-flavored granola

Preheat the broiler. Place the pound cake in a large bowl. Melt 2 tablespoons (28 g) of the butter and drizzle over the pound cake, tossing to coat evenly. Spread the pound cake on a sheet pan in an even layer. Broil for 2 minutes, until browned, turning to toast all sides. In a large skillet, melt the remaining 3 tablespoons (42 g) butter, add the nectarines, and cook over medium-high heat, stirring occasionally, until the nectarines are soft. Add the brown sugar and stir to melt. Remove from the heat, stir in the bourbon, vanilla vodka, ginger, and balsamic vinegar. Carefully ignite the alcohol and stir with a long-handled, heatproof spoon until the flame subsides. Place over medium heat, cooking until thickened. Remove from the heat, add the blackberries, and stir to combine. Scoop ice cream into 6 individual bowls and top with the nectarines and syrup. Add the toasted pound cake and sprinkle with the granola.

Prep = 30 minutes **Broil** = 2 minutes **Yield** = 6 servings

Cherries Jubilee
with Chambord

Borrowed from a recipe I found from Seafarers' Yacht Club in Annapolis, Maryland, this delightful dessert is packed with flavor. The chocolate liqueur is the secret to the flavorful punch of the cherries and sauce. Impress any guests by making this in front of them as a grand finale to any dinner. Note: Use *extreme* caution when flambéing!

1 (15-ounce [428 g]) can pitted Bing cherries in syrup
1 (14½-ounce [412 g]) can pitted tart cherries in water
2 tablespoons (16 g) cornstarch
¼ cup (50 g) granulated sugar
½ teaspoon ground allspice
¼ cup (60 ml) black raspberry liqueur, such as Chambord
¼ cup (60 ml) brandy
6 tablespoons (90 ml) chocolate liqueur, such as Godiva
1 quart (570 g) vanilla ice cream

Combine the Bing and tart cherries in a medium saucepan over medium heat, reserving 6 tablespoons (90 ml) of the Bing cherry syrup. Mix the cornstarch with the reserved syrup. Stir together the sugar and allspice, add to the cherry mixture, and bring to a boil. Lower the heat to a simmer, add the cornstarch mixture, and cook, stirring constantly, until thickened, 2 to 3 minutes. Remove from the heat and add the raspberry liqueur and brandy. Using a long match or flame wand, carefully light the brandy at the side of the pan to burn away the alcohol. Return to the heat and cook over medium heat, stirring constantly, for an additional minute. Place 1 tablespoon (15 ml) chocolate liqueur in the bottom of 6 serving bowls, top with the ice cream, pour the cherry mixture over the ice cream, and serve.

Prep = 10 minutes **Cook** = 5 minutes **Yield** = 6 servings

Irish Cream and Nut Blondies

Here, a basic recipe for classic blondies is enhanced by the combination of two complementary liqueurs, macadamia nuts, and white chocolate.

 8   tablespoons (1 stick, or 112 g) unsalted butter, softened
 1   cup (225 g) packed light brown sugar
 3   eggs
 ½   teaspoon pure vanilla extract
 2   teaspoons coffee liqueur
 1   tablespoon (15 ml) Irish cream liqueur
 1½ cups (165 g) all-purpose flour
 ¾   cup (82 g) coarsely chopped macadamia nuts
 4   ounces (115 g) white chocolate chips

Preheat the oven to 350ºF (180ºC, or gas mark 4). Butter an 8-inch (20.5 cm) square baking pan. In the bowl of a stand mixer fitted with the paddle attachment, beat the butter and sugar until creamy and smooth, about 7 minutes. Add the eggs one at a time, beating well after each addition. Add the vanilla, coffee liqueur, and Irish cream and blend well. Add the flour and blend until combined. Remove the bowl from the mixer and fold in the nuts and chocolate chips. Scrape the batter into the prepared pan and bake for 40 to 50 minutes, until a toothpick inserted into the center comes out clean. Transfer to a cooling rack and let cool completely, cut into 16 squares, and serve.

Prep = 15 minutes **Bake** = 40 to 50 minutes **Yield** = 16 squares

Irish Cream Cheesecake with Chocolate Mint Crust

Irish cream is one of those liqueurs that however mixed or served is simply dessert in a glass. Well you need something to go along with that drinkable dessert, so how about … dessert? This cheesecake also contains crème de menthe, providing a subtle layer of mint throughout.

CRUST:

- 1¼ cups (125 g) ground chocolate mint wafer cookies
- 1 tablespoon (13 g) granulated sugar
- 4 tablespoons (½ stick, or 55 g) unsalted butter, melted

FILLING:

- 6 ounces (170 g) bittersweet chocolate, chopped
- ¼ cup (60 ml) Irish cream liqueur
- 1 pound (455 g) cream cheese, softened
- ¾ cup (150 g) granulated sugar
- ½ cup (120 g) sour cream
- 1 tablespoon (15 ml) pure vanilla extract
- 1 tablespoon (15 ml) clear crème de menthe liqueur
- 4 extra-large eggs, at room temperature

Preheat the oven to 325°F (170°C, or gas mark 3). Butter the sides and bottom of a 9-inch (23 cm) round springform pan.

For the crust: Using a fork, stir together the cookie crumbs and sugar. Add the melted butter, stirring to moisten the cookie mixture. Pour into the prepared pan and press evenly along the bottom and halfway up the sides. Cover and refrigerate until ready to use.

For the filling: Place the chocolate in a mixing bowl. Heat the Irish cream over medium heat until just boiling. Pour over the chocolate and let stand for 5 minutes. Stir to combine and set aside. In the bowl of a stand mixer fitted with the paddle attachment, beat the cream cheese until creamy and smooth, about 5 minutes. Add the sugar and sour cream, beating until smooth and creamy, about 7 minutes. Add the vanilla, crème de menthe, and 1 egg, beating until the egg is thoroughly incorporated and the mixture is smooth. Scrape the sides of the bowl and paddle, add another egg, and beat until creamy and smooth. Add the remaining 2 eggs one at a time, beating very well after the addition of each. Pour half the batter into a heatproof bowl and add the chocolate mixture, stirring to combine evenly. (Place the bowl over a pot of boiling water if necessary, to stir until smooth.) Pour the chocolate mixture into the prepared crust. Pour the remaining white filling mixture over the chocolate and, using a dinner knife, swirl the two together, making a marbled effect. Place in the oven and bake for 45 to 50 minutes, until set. Transfer to a cooling rack. When at room temperature, remove the sides of the pan, cover, and refrigerate for at least 2 hours or overnight. Serve.

Prep = 30 minutes **Bake** = 45 to 50 minutes
Chill = at least 2 hours **Yield** = 10 servings

Coconut Rum and Pineapple Cheesecake

If you can't get to the islands, bring the islands to you. Take yourself on a culinary vacation in the middle of the winter by combining the flavors of the islands in this tempting cheesecake.

CRUST:

2	cups (200 g) graham cracker crumbs
1	tablespoon (13 g) granulated sugar
1/2	cup (40 g) toasted flaked coconut
1/4	cup (41 g) finely chopped, toasted macadamia nuts
3	tablespoons (42 g) unsalted butter, melted

FILLING:

3	(8-ounce [225 g]) packages cream cheese, softened
1 1/4	cups (295 g) sour cream
1	cup (200 g) granulated sugar
4	eggs
1	cup (80 g) toasted shredded coconut
2	tablespoons (28 ml) coconut-flavored rum
1	(20-ounce [570 g]) can crushed pineapple, drained

PINEAPPLE CURD:

1/2	cup (100 g) granulated sugar
1 1/2	teaspoons cornstarch
1	(20-ounce [570 g]) can crushed pineapple in syrup
3	whole eggs
2	egg yolks
2	tablespoons (30 ml) heavy cream
2	teaspoons spiced rum
2	tablespoons (28 g) unsalted butter, cut into small pieces, at room temperature

1/2	cup (63 g) toasted and chopped macadamia nuts, for garnish

Preheat the oven to 375°F (190°C, or gas mark 5).

For the crust: Combine the graham cracker crumbs with the sugar, coconut, macadamia nuts, and butter, tossing with a fork until evenly moistened. Pour the mixture into a 9-inch (23 cm) round springform pan, pressing evenly into the bottom and 2 inches (5 cm) up the sides of the pan. Cover and refrigerate until ready to use.

For the filling: In the bowl of a stand mixer fitted with the paddle attachment, beat the cream cheese until smooth and creamy. Add the sour cream and beat until there are no lumps and it is smooth and creamy. Beat in the sugar, then add the eggs one at a time, beating well after the addition of each and scraping the sides and bottom of the bowl. Add the coconut, coconut rum, and pineapple, and beat on low to just combine. Pour the mixture into the prepared crust, place on the center rack of the oven, and bake for 1 hour and 10 minutes, until the top is golden and the cake is firm. Transfer to a cooling rack to cool for 30 minutes. Remove the sides from the pan, cover the cake with plastic wrap, and refrigerate for at least 2 hours and up to overnight.

For the pineapple curd: In a saucepan, whisk together the sugar and cornstarch. Add the pineapple and place the pan over medium-high heat. Cook, stirring, until combined and thickened. Remove from the heat and whisk in the eggs one at a time, mixing after each addition. Add the heavy cream, egg yolks, rum, and butter in little bits at a time, stirring vigorously to blend. Once combined, transfer the curd to a container and cover tightly with plastic wrap directly touching the top of the curd. Refrigerate at least 1 hour and up to overnight. When the cheesecake is ready to serve, remove from the refrigerator, spread the top with an even layer of pineapple curd, sprinkle with an even layer of toasted macadamia nuts, slice, and serve.

Prep = 30 minutes **Bake** = 1 hour and 10 minutes
Chill = at least 2 hours **Yield** = 12 servings

Orange-Rum Pumpkin Pie

Pumpkin, which can be on the bland side even when spiced, definitely perks up with the addition of rum and orange liqueur.

CRUST:

2 ½	cups (275 g) all-purpose flour
2	tablespoons (25 g) granulated sugar
1 ½	teaspoons salt
	Pinch of ground nutmeg
16	tablespoons (2 sticks, or 225 g) unsalted butter, chilled, cut into cubes
6 to 7	tablespoons (90 to 105 ml) ice water

FILLING:

1 ⅔	cups (375 g) pumpkin purée
1	tablespoon (18 g) orange marmalade
1	tablespoon (15 ml) dark spiced rum
1	tablespoon (15 ml) orange liqueur, such as Cointreau
2	tablespoons (40 g) honey
3	eggs
1	egg yolk
½	teaspoon ground cloves
¼	teaspoon ground nutmeg
½	teaspoon ground cinnamon
¾	cup (175 ml) heavy cream

For the crust: In the bowl of a food processor fitted with the blade attachment, combine the flour, sugar, salt, and nutmeg, and pulse a couple of times to mix. Add the butter and pulse 20 to 25 times, just until the dough has a grainy cornmeal consistency. Add 5 tablespoons (75 ml) of cold water and pulse until the dough comes into a ball in the bowl. If more water is needed, add 1 teaspoon at a time until the dough comes together. Transfer to a sheet of plastic wrap and press into a large disk, wrap, and refrigerate for at least 1 hour. When ready to roll out, preheat the oven to 400°F (200°C, or gas mark 6). Unwrap the dough and lay flat on a well-floured work surface. Using a rolling pin, roll the dough into a 20-inch (51 cm) -diameter disk, turning, flipping, and coating with flour as needed. Roll the dough onto the rolling pin and gently lay into a 9-inch (23 cm) deep-dish pie plate. Using your fingers, press the dough around the edge of the pie plate, pressing and squeezing into a fluted edge. Place a rack in the bottom third of the oven. Line the pie dough with foil and spread the bottom with pie weights, dried rice, or dried beans. Place the dough in the oven and bake for 20 minutes. Remove the foil and bake until the crust is golden brown, about 10 additional minutes. Transfer to a cooling rack, and lower the oven temperature to 350°F (180°C, or gas mark 4).

For the filling: In a large bowl, combine the pumpkin with the orange marmalade, spiced rum, orange liqueur, and honey, and stir to combine. Add the eggs and egg yolk, whisking well until smooth. Add the cloves, nutmeg, cinnamon, and heavy cream, and stir to combine. Pour the filling into the prebaked pie crust, place in the oven, and bake for 60 to 65 minutes, until a toothpick inserted into the center comes out clean. Let cool on a cooling rack and serve.

Prep = 30 minutes   **Bake** = 1½ hours   **Yield** = 10 servings

Pecan Caramel Popcorn with Spiced Rum

This is an addictive, tasty, popcorn treat—the spiced rum gives just the right subtle depth of spiciness to the popcorn that you won't find in caramel corn.

10	cups (500 g) plain popped popcorn
³⁄₄	cup (93 g) coarsely chopped toasted pecans
6	tablespoons (83 g) unsalted butter
2	cups (400 g) granulated sugar
2	tablespoons (30 ml) spiced rum

Preheat the oven to 300°F (150°C, or gas mark 2). Combine the popcorn and pecans in a large bowl and set aside. In a saucepan over medium-high heat, melt the butter, add the sugar, and cook, stirring periodically, for 5 minutes, until the sugar turns caramel brown in color. Remove from the heat and stir in the spiced rum, being careful of the rising steam. Pour the caramel over the popcorn, stirring quickly to coat evenly. Transfer the popcorn to a large sheet pan, place in the oven, and bake for 10 minutes, stir the popcorn, and bake for an additional 5 minutes. Remove from the oven and let cool. Break into pieces and serve, or store in an airtight container.

Prep = 10 minutes   **Cook** = 25 minutes   **Yield** = about 10 cups (500 g)

Irish Whiskey Cake with Dried Fruits and Nuts

This is almost like a fruitcake, but better. It is moist, tender, and delicious, packed with fruits and nuts and a rich whiskey glaze. Serve this beautiful dessert with coffee and Irish cream liquer.

1	cup (120 g) dried cranberries
1	cup (145 g) golden raisins
1	cup (235 ml) Irish whiskey
1 ½	cups (165 g) all-purpose flour
1	teaspoon baking powder
½	teaspoon salt
½	teaspoon ground cinnamon
½	teaspoon ground nutmeg
¼	teaspoon ground cloves
12	tablespoons (1 ½ sticks, or 167 g) unsalted butter, softened
1	cup (225 g) packed brown sugar
3	eggs
2	tablespoons (14 g) grated lemon zest
2	tablespoons (14 g) grated orange zest
¾	cup (92 g) chopped almonds

GLAZE:

2	cups (475 ml) heavy cream
¼	cup (60 ml) Irish cream liqueur
¼	cup (25 g) confectioners' sugar
½	teaspoon ground cinnamon

Preheat the oven to 350°F (180°C, or gas mark 4). Butter and flour a 10-inch (25.5 cm) tube cake pan and set aside. Place the cranberries and raisins in a bowl and top with the whiskey; set aside to macerate for 20 minutes. In a bowl, whisk together the flour, baking powder, salt, cinnamon, nutmeg, and cloves until combined, then set aside. In the bowl of a stand mixer fitted with the paddle attachment, beat the butter and brown sugar until smooth and creamy, about 5 minutes. Add the eggs one at a time, blending well after each addition. Add the flour mixture and the fruit and whiskey mixture a little at a time, alternating between the two, beginning and ending with the flour. Blend well after each addition. Scrape the sides of the bowl and the paddle and blend to combine. Add the zests and the almonds, and blend to just combine. Scrape the batter into the prepared pan. Bake on the center rack of the oven for 40 to 50 minutes, until a toothpick inserted into the center comes out clean. Transfer to a cooling rack and let cool for 10 minutes. Invert the cake, releasing it from the pan, and then invert again onto a serving plate.

For the glaze: In a bowl, combine the cream with the liqueur, confectioners' sugar, and cinnamon, stirring with a fork. Once the cake has cooled, pour the glaze over it, slice, and serve.

Prep = 35 minutes **Bake** = 40 to 50 minutes **Yield** = 10 servings

Whiskey Pecan Drop Candies

In Texas these are called pralines. I call them good. When you try them, you will taste the layers of flavor. There are truly layers in a bite: first sweet (sugar), then nutty (pecans), then caramel oak (whiskey), with a hint of vanilla.

- ½ cup (112 g) packed light brown sugar
- ¾ cup (150 g) granulated sugar
- ½ cup (120 g) sour cream
- 1 teaspoon pure vanilla extract
- 2 tablespoons (30 ml) sour mash whiskey
- 1 cup (100 g) pecan halves

In a saucepan, stir together the sugars and the sour cream over medium heat until the mixture reaches the soft ball stage, about 10 minutes. When a candy thermometer registers 240°F (115.5°C). Add the vanilla and whiskey, stir, and remove from the heat. Stir in the pecans. Let sit for 3 minutes, stir, and then drop by the tablespoon onto waxed paper. Let cool and harden, about 2 hours. Wrap and store in a dry place.

Prep = 10 minutes **Cook** = 15 minutes **Cool** = 2 hours
Yield = 12 candies

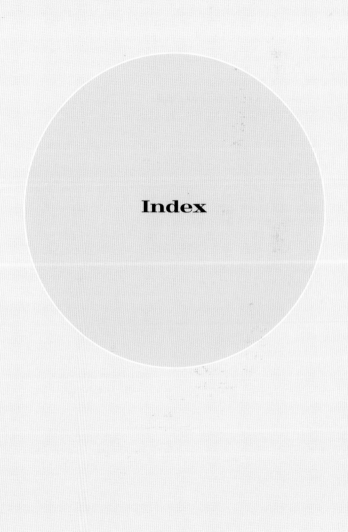

Index

C

About the Author

A graduate of Johnson & Wales University School of Culinary Arts, Dwayne Ridgaway has practiced his trade for more than twenty years as a chef, caterer, consultant, food stylist, and author. He currently resides in Bristol, Rhode Island, where he spends much of his time working and consulting in the hotel, food, and event design industries. He is author of several other books, including *Lasagna: The Art of Layered Cooking*; *Pizza: 50 Traditional and Alternative Recipes for the Oven and the Grill*; *Cast Iron Cooking: 50 Gourmet-Quality Dishes from Entrees to Desserts*; and *The Gourmet's Guide to Cooking with Chocolate*.

Acknowledgments

I have so many people to thank for their support and generosity in the development of my books. I truly enjoy every minute of the creative and practical process of creating a cookbook—from the instructional and educational material to the cooking and design of recipes. I have so many influences along the way. My supportive family and passionate friends are always there to give me input and true critique of my material—whether it be the collaboration process with my good friend Cliff or the testing parties with Steve and Erin. I am always including my friends along the way for real opinions. My cooking is a style that is creative and inspired. I can be motivated by the produce shelves in the market; or by a friend's dish at a dinner party; by a story from past family recipes; or by a recent trip I have just returned from. But most of all, I am inspired to create dishes that I know everyone will enjoy—dishes that are simple to prepare and delicious to eat. I owe this style to all of my friends who enjoy gathering in the kitchen at my home every time I extend an invitation. It is difficult to name them all, but they, as always, know who they are.

Thanks are, of course, due to my publishing family at Rockport Publishers and Quarry Books, who make these exquisite books possible.

FREE PUBLIC LIBRARY UNION, NEW JERSEY

3 9549 00479 5671